FLASHMAPS

CHICAGO

Editorial Updater
Julie S. Burros

Cartographic Updater
Mapping Specialists

Proofreader
Susan Gryder

Editor
Robert Blake

Cover Design
Chie Ushio

Creative Director
Fabrizio La Rocca

Cartographer
David Lindroth

Designer
Tigist Getachew

Production Manager
Angela L. McLean

Cartographic Contributors
Edward Faherty
Sheila Levin
Page Lindroth
Eric Rudolph

Fodor's

Fodor's Travel Publications
New York, Toronto, London, Sydney, Auckland

Contents

ESSENTIAL INFORMATION	MAP
Important Telephone Numbers	iv–v
Northeast Illinois	1
Chicagoland	2
Chicago	3
Streetfinder/Downtown	4
Streetfinder/North Side	5
Zip Codes	6
Neighborhoods	7
Hospitals & 24-Hour Pharmacies	8
McCormick Place	9
Consulates	10
Libraries	11
Universities, Colleges & Schools	12
University of Chicago	13
Illinois Institute of Technology	14
Northwestern University	15

TRANSPORTATION	MAP
Midway Airport	16
O'Hare International Airport	17
Buses/Near North	18
Buses/Downtown & Loop	19
CTA/Area	20
CTA/Near North	21
CTA/Downtown & Loop	22
Metra/ Northern Suburbs	23
Metra/ Western & Southern Suburbs	24
Driving & Parking	25

EXPLORING	MAP
Top Attractions	26
Architecture	27
Oak Park	28
Hyde Park & Kenwood	29
Evanston	30
Skokie	31
Bronzeville	32
Churches, Temples & Mosques	33
Museums	34
John G Shedd Aquarium	35

EXPLORING (cont.)

	MAP
Art Institute of Chicago	36
Field Museum	37
Museum of Science and Industry	38
Art Galleries	39

PARKS & RECREATION

	MAP
Beaches	40
Parks	41
Lincoln Park	42
Lincoln Park Zoo	43
Stadiums & Arenas	44
Public Golf Courses	45

SHOPPING

	MAP
Shopping/Near North & Loop	46
Shopping/North Side	47

DINING & LODGING

	MAP
Restaurants/Downtown	48
Restaurants/Near North	49
Restaurants/North Side, Bucktown & Wicker Park	50
Restaurants/South Side	51
Hotels/O'Hare Airport Area	52
Hotels/Greater Chicago	53

NIGHTLIFE

	MAP
Performing Arts	54
Movies	55
Nightlife/Near North & Downtown	56
Nightlife/North Side	57

Special Sales

Fodor's Travel Publications are available at special discounts for bulk purchases for sales promotions or premiums. Special editions, including personalized covers, excerpts of existing guides, and corporate imprints, can be created in large quantities for special needs. For more information, contact your local bookseller or write to Special Markets/Premium Sales, 1745 Broadway, MD 6-2, New York, NY 10019, or e-mail special markets@randomhouse.com.

ISBN 978-1-4000-1630-3   **ISSN 1532-7213**

PRINTED IN CHINA 10 9 8 7 6 5 4 3 2 1

Area Codes: All (312) unless otherwise noted.

EMERGENCIES

AAA Emergency ☎ 866/968-7222

ACLU ☎ 201-9740

Ambulance/Fire/Police ☎ 911

Chicago Animal Control ☎ 747-1406

Coast Guard Calumet Harbor Search and Rescue ☎ 773/768-4093

Dental Referral ☎ 800/336-8478

Domestic Violence Help Line ☎ 773/278-4566

Illinois AIDS/HIV/STD Hotline ☎ 800/342-2437

Illinois Poison Center ☎ 800/942-5969

Medical Referral Service ☎ 670-2550

National Runaway Switchboard ☎ 800/621-4000

Osco 24-hour Pharmacies ☎ 877/728-6655

Rape Crisis Line ☎ 888/293-2080

Towed Cars ☎ 744-PARK

Travelers Aid ☎ 773/894-2427

Walgreens 24-hour Pharmacies ☎ 877/250-5823

Youth Crisis Hotline ☎ 800/448-4663

SERVICES

AAA ☎ 866/968-7222

Alcoholics Anonymous ☎ 312/346-1475

Attorney General's Office ☎ 814-3580

Better Business Bureau ☎ 832-0500

Board of Elections ☎ 269-7900

Chicago Area Gay & Lesbian Chamber of Commerce ☎ 773/303-0167

Chicago City Services ☎ 311

Chicago Convention and Tourism Bureau ☎ 567-8500

Chicago Dept. of Public Health ☎ 747-9884

Chicago Visitor Information ☎ 877/CHICAGO

Consumer Services ☎ 744-4006

Cook County Commission on Human Rights ☎ 603-1100

Department on Aging ☎ 744-4016

Gay and Lesbian Helpline ☎ 773/929-4357

Gay and Lesbian Anti-Violence Project ☎ 773/871-2273

Illinois Relay Center ☎ 711

Mayor's Office for People with Disabilities ☎ 744-7050

Mayor's Office of Special Events ☎ 744-3315

Police/Fire Non-Emergency ☎ 311

Traffic Court ☎ 603-2941

U.S. Postal Service ☎ 800/275-8777

TRANSPORTATION

Airport Express ☎ 888/2THEVAN

American United Cab Co. ☎ 773/248-7600

Amtrak ☎ 800/872-7245

Checker Taxi ☎ 243-2537

Chicago Transit Authority Customer Service ☎ 888/YOUR-CTA

Flash Cab ☎ 773/866-9200

O'Hare International Airport ☎ 773/686-2200 / 800/832-6352

Greyhound ☎ 800/231-2222

Greyhound Bus Terminal ☎ 408-5800

Metra ☎ 322-6777

Midway Airport ☎ 773/838-0600

Omega Airport Shuttle ☎ 773/734-6688

Paratransit Information ☎ 800/606-1282

RTA Travel Information ☎ 836-7000

Wheelchair Accessible Cabs ☎ 800/281-4466

Yellow Cab Co. ☎ 829-4222

ENTERTAINMENT

Broadway In Chicago ☎ 977-1700

Chicago Cultural Center ☎ 346-3278

Chicago Dance & Music Alliance Performance Hotline ☎ 987-1123

Chicago Live Concert Hotline ☎ 666-6667

Chicago Sinfonietta ☎ 236-3681

Chicago Symphony Orchestra ☎ 800/223-7114

Civic Orchestra ☎ 294-3420

Area Codes: All (312) unless otherwise noted.

Grant Park Music Festival
☎ 742-7638

Jazz Hotline ☎ 427-3300

Lyric Opera ☎ 332-2244

Moviefone ☎ 444-FILM

Ticketmaster ☎ 559-1212,
☎ 902-1500 (Arts line)

PARKS AND RECREATION

Brookfield Zoo ☎ 800/201-0784

Chicago Botanic Garden
☎ 847/835-5440

Chicago Motor Speedway
☎ 773/242-2277

Chicago Park District ☎ 742-PLAY

Chicago Park District Golf Info
☎ 245-0909

Chicago River Canoe & Kayak
☎ 773/252-3307

Chicago Rowing Foundation
☎ 482-8984

Chicago Sailing Club ☎ 773/871-7245

Chicago Sport Fishing Association
☎ 922-1100

Chicagoland Bicycle Federation
☎ 427-3325

Forest Preserves of Cook County
☎ 800/870-3666

Garfield Park Conservatory
☎ 746-5100

Lincoln Park Zoo ☎ 742-2000

Millenium Park Hotline ☎ 742-1168

Navy Pier ☎ 595-PIER

SPECTATOR SPORTS

Arlington Park Race Track
☎ 847/385-7500

Chicago Bears ☎ 847/615-BEAR

Chicago Blackhawks ☎ 455-7000

Chicago Bulls ☎ 455-4000

Chicago Cubs ☎ 800/THE CUBS

Chicago Fire ☎ 888/657-3473

Chicago Rush ☎ 773/243-3434

Chicago Sky ☎ 828-9550

Chicago White Sox ☎ 559-1212 /
866/SOX-GAME

Chicago Wolves ☎ 800/THE WOLVES

Northwestern Wildcats
☎ 847/491-2287

United Center ☎ 455-4500

TOURS

Walking Tours:

Bike Chicago ☎ 888/BIKE-WAY

Bobby's Bike Hike ☎ 915-0995

Chicago Architecture Foundation
☎ 922-TOUR

Chicago Greeters ☎ 744-8000

Chicago History Museum
☎ 642-4600

**Chicago History Museum
Neighorhood Walking Tours**
☎ 642-4600

Chicago Neighborhood Tours
☎ 742-1190

Chicago Supernatural Tours
☎ 708/499-0300

**Frank Lloyd Wright Home and
Studio Foundation of Oak Park**
☎ 708/848-1978

Herb's Downtown Tours
☎ 773/404-2400

Segway Tours ☎ 800/209-3370

Shopwalks Shopping Tours
☎ 773/255-7866

Walk Chicago Tours ☎ 708/557-5400

Wrigley Field Tours ☎ 773/404-2827

Boat Tours:

**Chicago Architecture Foundation
River Cruise** ☎ 922-TOUR

Chicago From the Lake ☎ 527-2002

Mercury Chicago Skyline Cruiseline
☎ 332-1353

Odyssey Cruises ☎ 888/957-2327

Wendella Sightseeing Boats
☎ 337-1446

Bus Tours:

American Sightseeing ☎ 251-3100

Black CouTours ☎ 773/233-8907

Chicago Grayline ☎ 251-3107

**Chicago Trolley Company /
Double Decker Tours**
☎ 773/648-5000

Tour Black Chicago
☎ 773/684-9034

Untouchable Tours ☎ 773/881-1195

Art Tours:

Art Excursions ☎ 630/671-9745

Art on the Move Tours
☎ 847/432-6265

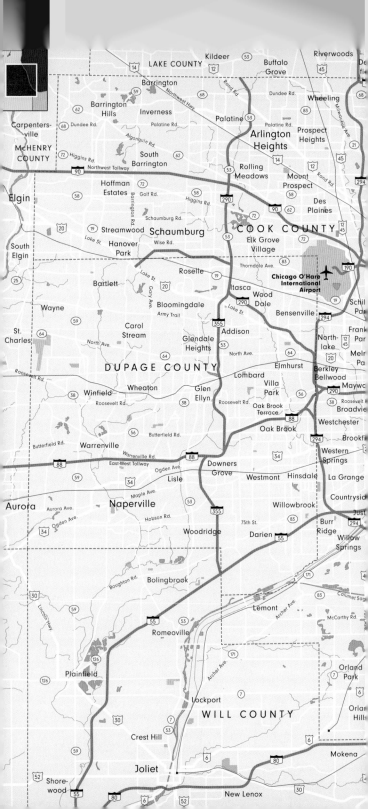

MAP 3 **Chicago**

Oakton St.
Lee St.
Touhy Ave.
Wolf Rd.
294
Des Rd.
Rand Rd.
21
43
Oakton Ave.
14
Howard St.
Carpenter Rd.
50
90
72

PARK RIDGE
Devon Ave.
Canfield St.
Touhy Ave.
43
Milwaukee Ave.
Northwest Hwy.
Caldwell Ave.
W Devon Ave.
94
14
North Br.

72
W Talcott Ave.
90
21
W Higgins Rd.

190
Chicago O'Hare
International
Airport
12
45
East River Rd.
Lawrence Ave.
W Lawrence Ave.

NORRIDGE
HARWOOD HEIGHTS

19
Forest Preserve
Des Plaines River Rd.
Forest Preserve Ave.
43
19
W Irving Park Rd.
W Addison Ave.
W Belmont Ave.
N Cicero Ave.

25th St.
FRANKLIN PARK
ELMWOOD PARK
N Harlem Ave.
N Oak Park Ave.
N Narragansett Ave.
N Austin Ave.
W Diversey Ave.
N Central Ave.
N Laramie Ave.
W Grand Ave.

Grand Ave.
Wolf Rd.
294
Mannheim Rd.
25th St.
NORTHLAKE
64
20
Lake St.
12/20
45
MELROSE PARK
North Ave.
64
OAK PARK
290
St. Charles Rd.
5th St.
Division St.
Chicago Ave.
Lake St.
Butterfield Rd.
Madison St.
25th St.
17th St.
9th St.
Lathrop
Madison
Washington Blvd.
Madison
290
Des Plaines River
Columbus Park
Eisenhower Expwy.

38
Roosevelt Rd.
43
BERWYN
16th St.
50

Cermak Rd.
Salt Cr.
Harlem Ave.
Oak Park
Ridgeland Ave.
Ogden Ave.
CICERO

31st St.
Forest Preserve
Ogden Ave.
36
Despaines
Pershing Rd.
55
WESTERN SPRINGS
12/20
45
47th St.
171
Chicago Sanitary & Ship Canal
Adlai E. Stevenson Expwy.
S Archer Ave.

County Line Rd.
55th St.
Willow Springs Rd.
Plainfield Rd.
LaGrange Rd.
MCCOOK
171
S Harlem Ave.
Midway Airport

SUMMIT
Joliet Rd.
55
171
S Cicero Ave.
50
BEDFORD PARK

294
Wolf Rd.
55
Archer Ave.
Roberts Rd.
43
BURR RIDGE
294
BURBANK

MAP

3

N

0   2 miles
0   2 km

Oakton Ave.

N Rogers St.

LINCOLN-
WOOD

W Touhy Ave.

41

W Pratt Blvd.

W Devon Ave.

W Peterson St.   14

Legion
Park

Chicago R.

W Foster St.   41

Lincoln
Park

W Lawrence Ave.

Lake Michigan

W Montrose Ave.

W Montrose Ave.

Horner
Park   19

N Lincoln Ave.

Wrigley
Field

W Addison Ave.

90
94

W Belmont Ave.

N Damen Ave.

N Ashland Ave.

N Clark St.

41

W Fullerton Ave.

Theater on the Lake

Lincoln
Park

W Armitage Ave.

N Clybourn Ave.

N Halsted St.

Lincoln
Park
Zoo

W North Ave.   64

Humboldt
Park

N Western Ave.

N California Ave.

W Division St.

N State St.

W Chicago Ave.

Lake Shore Dr.

W Grand Ave.

N Elston Ave.

N Milwaukee Ave.

N Pulaski Ave.

N Grand Ave.

Garfield
Park

Washington Blvd.
W Madison St.

Union
Station

90
94

Sears
Tower

Chicago Art Institute

290

University of Illinois
at Chicago

Grant Park

Shedd
Aquarium

Douglas
Park

CHICAGO

Adler Planetarium

Field Museum of Natural History
Soldier Field

W Ogden Ave.

W 18th St.

S Michigan Ave.

W Cermak Rd.

S Blue Island Ave.

South Br. Chicago R.

W 26th St.   55

41

W 31st St.

W 31st St.

S Kedzie Ave.

S California Ave.

S Archer Ave.

W 35th St.

U.S. Cellular
Field

Dr. Martin Luther King Jr. Dr.

S Indiana Ave.

Adlai E. Stevenson Expwy.

W Pershing Rd.

S Halsted St.

Lake Shore Dr.

W 47th St.

Sherman
Park

W 51st St.

Washington
Park

Drexel Blvd.

W Garfield Blvd.

W 55th St.

University
of Chicago

Museum of Science
and Industry

S Kedzie Rd.

S Western Ave.

S Ashland Ave.

S Damen Ave.

Racine Ave.

W 59th St.

Midway
Plaisance

Jackson
Park

Marquette
Park

W 63rd St.

E 63rd St.

Dr. Martin

W 67th St.

E 67th St.

South Shore
Golf Course

W 71st St.

Chicago Skyway

E 71st St.

41

S Pulaski Rd.

Columbus St.

W 79th St.

S State St.

Luther King Jr. Dr.

E 75th St.

Exchange Ave.

South Shore Dr.

Rainbow
Park

W 83rd St.

94

E 79th St.

90

E 83rd St.

MAP 4 **Streetfinder/Downtown**

Letter codes refer to grid sectors on preceding map

NORTH-SOUTH STREETS
(N prefix north of Madison; S prefix south of Madison)

Aberdeen St A2, A3
Archer Ave A6, B5
Astor St B1
Benton Pl B3
Blue Island Ave A5
Branch St A1, A2
Calumet Ave C5, C6
Cambridge Ave A2
Canal Port A6, B5
Canal St B3, B6
Carpenter St A2, A6
Cherry Ave A1
Clark St B1, B6
Cleveland Ave B1, B2
Clybourn Ave A1, B1
Columbus Dr C3, C5
Cottage Grove Ave C6
Crosby St A1, A2
Dan Ryan Expwy A2, B6
Dearborn St B1, B6
Desplaines St A2, A6
Dewitt Pl C2
Fairbanks Ct C2, C3
Federal St B4, B6
Field Blvd C3
Franklin St B1, B4
Green St A2, A4
Halsted St A1, A6
Hickory Ave A1, A2
Hooker St A1, A2
Hudson Ave B1, B2
Indiana Ave C5, C6
Jefferson St A3, A5
JFK Expwy A2
Kingsbury St A1, B3
Lake Shore Dr C1, C6
Larrabee St. A1, A2
LaSalle St B1, B4
Lumber St A6, B5
McClurg Ct C2, C3
Michigan Ave C2, C6
Miller St A4
Milwaukee Ave A2, B3
ML King Jr Dr C6
Mohawk St A1
Newbury St A5
Ogden Ave A2, B1
Orleans St B1, B3
Park Ave B1
Peoria St A2, A6
Plymouth Ct B4
Prairie Ave C5, C6
Princeton Ave B6
Rush St B1, C2
St Clair St C2
Sangamon St A2, A6

Sedgwick St B1, B2
Silverton Way C6
State Pkwy B1
State St B1, B6
Stetson Ave C3
Stevenson Expwy A6, C6
Stewart Ave B6
Union Ave A2, A6
Wabash Ave B2, B6
Wacker Dr B4, C3
Wells St B1, B5
Wentworth Ave B6

EAST-WEST STREETS
(W prefix west of State St; E prefix east of State St)

11th St B4, C4
12th St A5
13th St A5, C5
14th Pl A5, B5
14th St A5, C5
16th St A5, C5
17th St A5, B5
18th Pl A5
18th St A5, C5
19th St A5, B5
21st St A6, C6
22nd Pl B6
23rd Pl B6, C6
23rd St B6, C6
24th Pl B6
24th St B6, C6
25th Pl B6
25th St A6, C6
26th St A6, C6
8th St B4, C4
9th St B4, C4
Adams St A3, C3
Alexander St B6
Balbo Dr B4, C4
Banks St B1
Barber St A5
Bellevue Pl B1, C1
Blackhawk St A1, B1
Burton Pl B1
Carroll Ave A3
Cedar St B1, C1
Cermak Rd. A6, C6
Chestnut St A2, C2
Chicago Ave A2, C2
Congress Pkwy B4, C4
Couch Pl B3
Court Pl B3
Cullerton St A6, C6
Delaware Pl B2, C2
Depot St A5, B5
Division St A1, C1
Eastman Ave A1

Eisenhower Expwy A4, B4
Elm St A1, C1
Erie St A2, C2
Evergreen Ave A1, B1
Fry St A2
Fulton St A3, B3
Goethe St B1, C1
Grand Ave A2, C2
Haddock Pl B3, C3
Harrison Ave A4, C4
Hill St B1
Hobbie St A1
Hubbard St A2, C3
Huron St A2, C2
Institute Pl B2
Jackson Blvd A4, C4
Jackson Dr C4
Kinzie St A3, C3
Lake St A3, C3
Liberty St A5
Locust St B2
Madison St A3, C3
Maple St B1
Marble Pl B3
Maxwell St A5, B5
McFetridge Dr C5
Monroe Dr C3
Monroe St A3, C3
N Water St C3
North Ave A1, B1
North Blvd B1
O'Brien St A5
Oak St A2, C2
Ohio St A2, C2
Ontario St B2, C2
Pearson St B2, C2
Polk St A4, B4
Randolph St A3, C3
Roosevelt Rd A5, C5
S Water St C3
Schiller St B1
Scott St B1, C1
Solidarity Dr C5
Superior St A2, C2
Taylor St A4, B4
Van Buren St A4, C4
Waldron Dr C5
Walton St B2, C2
Washington Blvd A3, C3
Weed St A1
Wendell St B1

Letter codes refer to grid sectors on preceding map

NORTH-SOUTH STREETS
(*N prefix north of Madison*)
Ashland Ave A1, A6
Beacon St B1, B2
Belmont Harbor Dr C3
Bissell St B5, B6
Bosworth Ave A2, A6
Broadway B1, C4
Burling St C4, C6
Cambridge Ave C4, C5
Cannon Dr C4, C5
Clarendon St B1, B3
Clark St A1, C6
Cleveland Ave C5, C6
Clifton Ave B2, B6
Clybourn Ave A4, B6
Commonwealth Ave C4, C5
Damen Ave A1, A6
Dayton St B2, B6
Dominick St A5, A6
Dover St A1, A2
Elaine Pl C3
Elston Ave A5,B6
Fremont St B3,B6
Geneva Ter C5
Glenwood Ave B1
Grant Pl C5
Greenview Ave A3, A6
Halsted St B3, B6
Hampden Ct C4, C5
Hazel St B2
Hermitage Ave A1, A6
Honore St A6
Howe St C6
Hudson Ave C5, C6
Janssen Ave A1, A5
Kenmore Ave B1, B6
Kingsbury St B6
Lake Shore Dr B1, C4
Lakeview Ave C4, C5
Lakewood Ave B3, B6
Larrabee St C5, C6
LaSalle St C6
Lincoln Ave A2, C6
Lincoln Park W C5, C6
Lister Ave A5
Magnolia Ave B1, B6
Malden St B1, B2
Marcey St B6
Marine Dr B1, C3
Marshfield Ave B3, B6
Maud Ave B6
Mendell St A6
Mildred Ave B4, B5
Mohawk St C6
Orchard St C4, C6
Orleans St C6
Park Ave C6

Paulina St A1, A6
Pine Grove Ave C3, C4
Racine Ave B1, B6
Ravenswood Ave A1, A4
Reta Ave B3
Sedgwick St C5, C6
Seminary Ave B3, B6
Sheffield Ave B3, B6
Sheridan Rd B1, C4
Simonds Dr C1
Surrey Ct B5
Throop St B6
Waterloo Ct C4
Wayne Ave B3, B5
Wells St C6
Wilton Ave B3, B5
Winchester Ave A1, A6
Winthrop Ave B1, B2
Wolcott Ave A1, A6
Wood St A6

EAST-WEST STREETS
(*W prefix west of State*)
Addison St A3, C3
Agatite Ave B2, C2
Ainslie St A1, B1
Aldine Ave B4, C4
Altgeld St A5, A5
Argyle St A1, B2
Arlington Pl C5
Armitage Ave A6, C6
Barry Ave A4, C4
Belden Ave A5, C5
Belle Plaine Ave A2, B2
Belmont Ave A4, C4
Bernice Ave A3
Berteau Ave A2
Bittersweet Pl C2
Bloomingdale Ave A6
Bradley Pl A3, B3
Briar Pl C4
Brompton Ave C3
Buckingham Pl B4, C4
Byron St A3, B3
Carmen Ave A1, B1
Castlewood Ter B1, C1
Concord Pl B6
Cornelia Ave A3, C3
Cortland St A6, B6
Cullom Ave A2, B2
Cuyler Ave A2, C2
Dakin St B3
Deming Pl C5
Dickens Ave A6, C6
Diversey Ave A4, C4
Drummond Pl C5
Eastwood Ave B1
Eddy St A3, B3
Eugenie St. C6

Fletcher St A4, B4
Foster Ave A1, B1
Fullerton Ave A5, C5
George St A4, B4
Gordon Ter C2
Grace St A3, C3
Grant Pl C5
Gunnison St B1
Hawthorne Pl C3
Henderson St A4, B4
Hutchinson St A2, C2
Irving Park Rd A3, C3
Junior Ave B2
Kemper Pl C5
Lakeside Ave B1, C1
Larchmont Ave A3
Lawrence Ave A1, C1
Lawrence Dr C1
Leland Ave A1, C1
Lill Ave A5, B5
Margate Ter B1
Melrose St A4, C4
Menomonee St C6
Montana Ave A5, B5
Montrose Ave A2, C2
Montrose Dr C2
Nelson St A4, B4
Newport Ave A3, C3
North Ave A6, C6
Oakdale Ave A4, C4
Patterson Ave A3, C3
Pensacola Ave A2, C2
Roscoe St A3,C4
Roslyn Pl C5
School St A4, B4
Schubert Ave B5, C5
St James Pl C5
St Paul Ave A6, C6
Stratford Pl C3
Sunnyside Ave A2, B2
Surf St C4
Wabansia Ave A6
Waveland Ave A3, C3
Webster Ave A5, C5
Wellington Ave A4, C4
Willow St B6, C6
Wilson Ave A2, C2
Wilson Dr C2
Windsor Ave B2
Winnemac Ave A1, B1
Winona St A1, B1
Wisconsin St B6, C6
Wolfram St A4, B4
Wrightwood Ave A5, C5

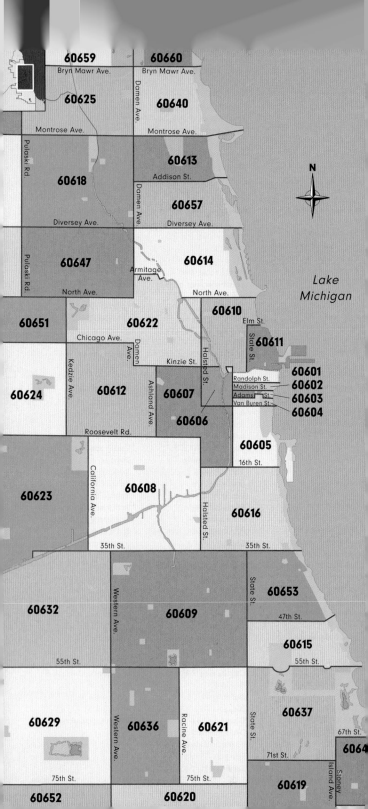

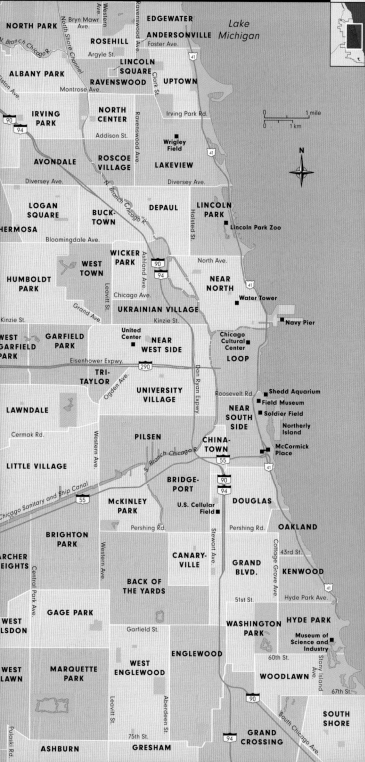

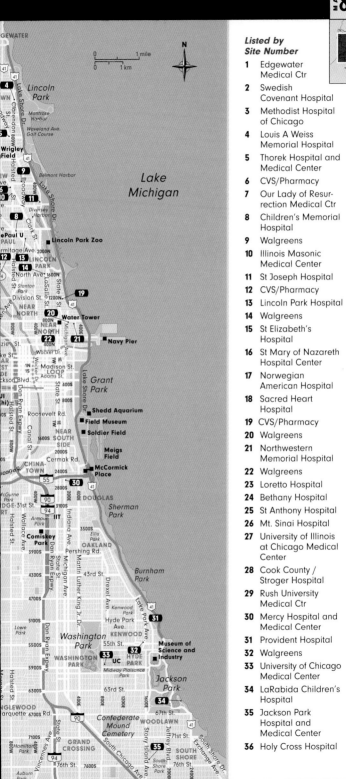

MAP 8

0 _____ 1 mile
0 _____ 1 km

Lake
Michigan

**Listed by
Site Number**

1   Edgewater
    Medical Ctr

2   Swedish
    Covenant Hospital

3   Methodist Hospital
    of Chicago

4   Louis A Weiss
    Memorial Hospital

5   Thorek Hospital and
    Medical Center

6   CVS/Pharmacy

7   Our Lady of Resur-
    rection Medical Ctr

8   Children's Memorial
    Hospital

9   Walgreens

10 Illinois Masonic
    Medical Center

11 St Joseph Hospital

12 CVS/Pharmacy

13 Lincoln Park Hospital

14 Walgreens

15 St Elizabeth's
    Hospital

16 St Mary of Nazareth
    Hospital Center

17 Norwegian
    American Hospital

18 Sacred Heart
    Hospital

19 CVS/Pharmacy

20 Walgreens

21 Northwestern
    Memorial Hospital

22 Walgreens

23 Loretto Hospital

24 Bethany Hospital

25 St Anthony Hospital

26 Mt. Sinai Hospital

27 University of Illinois
    at Chicago Medical
    Center

28 Cook County /
    Stroger Hospital

29 Rush University
    Medical Ctr

30 Mercy Hospital and
    Medical Center

31 Provident Hospital

32 Walgreens

33 University of Chicago
    Medical Center

34 LaRabida Children's
    Hospital

35 Jackson Park
    Hospital and
    Medical Center

36 Holy Cross Hospital

Listed Alphabetically

Bethany Hospital, 24.
3435 W Van Buren St
☎ 773/265-7700

Children's Memorial Hospital, 8.
707 W Fullerton Ave ☎ 773/880-4000

Cook County/Stroger Hospital, 36.
1901 W Harrison ☎ 864-6000

Edgewater Medical Center, 1.
5700 N Ashland Ave ☎ 773/878-6000

Holy Cross Hospital, 36.
2701 W 68th St ☎ 773/884-9000

Illinois Masonic Medical Center, 10.
836 W Wellington Ave ☎ 773/975-1600

Jackson Park Hospital and Medical Center, 35.
7531 S Stony Island Ave
☎ 773/947-7500

La Rabida Children's Hospital, 34.
E. 65th St and Lake Michigan
☎ 773/363-6700

Lincoln Park Hospital, 13.
550 W Webster Ave ☎ 773/883-2000

Loretto Hospital, 23.
645 S Central Ave ☎ 773/626-4300

Louis A Weiss Memorial Hospital, 4.
4646 N Marine Dr ☎ 773/878-8700

Mercy Hospital and Medical Center, 30.
2525 S Michigan Ave ☎ 567-2000

Methodist Hospital of Chicago, 3.
5025 N Paulina St ☎ 773/271-9040

Mt. Sinai Hospital, 26.
1500 S California Ave
☎ 773/542-2000

Norwegian American Hospital, 19.
1044 N Francisco Ave
☎ 773/292-8200

Our Lady of Resurrection Medical Center, 7.
5645 W Addison St ☎ 773/282-7000

Provident Hospital, 31.
500 E 51st St ☎ 572-2000

Rush University Medical Center, 29.
1653 W Congress Pkwy ☎ 942-5000

Sacred Heart Hospital, 18.
3240 W Franklin Blvd ☎ 773/722-3020

St Anthony Hospital, 25.
2875 W 19th St ☎ 773/484-1000

Saints Mary and Elizabeth Medical Center, 15.
St Elizabeth Campus
1431 N Claremont Ave
☎ 773/278-2000

St Joseph Hospital, 11.
2900 N Lake Shore Dr
☎ 773/665-3000

Saints Mary and Elizabeth Medical Center, 16.
St Mary Campus
2233 W Division St ☎ 770-2000

Swedish Covenant Hospital, 2.
5145 N California Ave
☎ 773/878-8200

Thorek Hospital and Medical Center, 5.
850 W Irving Park Rd
☎ 773/525-6780

University of Chicago Medical Center, 33.
5841 S Maryland Ave ☎ 773/702-1000

University of Illinois at Chicago Medical Center, 27.
1740 W Taylor St ☎ 996-7000

24-HOUR PHARMACIES

CVS/Pharmacy, 6.
3101 N Clark St ☎ 773/477-3333

CVS/Pharmacy, 12.
1714 N Sheffield ☎ 640-5161

CVS/Pharmacy, 19.
1201 N State St ☎ 640-2842

Walgreens, 9.
Broadway & Belmont Ave
☎ 773/327-3591

Walgreens, 14. 1601 N Wells St
☎ 642-4008

Walgreens, 20. 757 N Michigan Ave
☎ 664-8686

Walgreens, 32. 1554 E 55th St
☎ 773/667-1177

Walgreens, 22. 641 N Clark St
☎ 587-1416

E Cullerton St.

E 21st St.

E Cermak Rd.

North Building

S Calumet Ave.

Martin Luther King Jr. Dr.

S Lake Shore Dr.

41

S Lake Shore Dr.

41

Exhibition Halls

West Building

Hyatt Regency McCormick Place

Garage & Conference Center

E 23rd St.

S Calumet Ave.

Main Entrance

McCormick Square

Grand Concourse

Metra Station

M

Lakeside Center (East Building)

Exhibition Halls

South Building

Exhibition Halls

S Lake Shore Dr.

S Lake Shore Dr.

Arie Crown Theater

E 24th St.

55

55

E 25th St.

41

N

41

41

0   600 feet

0   200 meters

Listed by Site Number

1	Poland	11	Korea	20	Greece
2	China	12	Brazil	20	Spain
3	Croatia	13	Austria	21	Argentina
3	Japan	13	Great Britian	21	France
3	Switzerland	13	Ireland	22	Canada
4	Thailand	14	Egypt	23	Israel
5	Ukraine	14	Italy	24	Indonesia
6	Germany	15	Netherlands	25	Philippines
7	Denmark	16	Belgium	26	Australia
8	Greece	16	Pakistan	27	Haiti
9	Lithuania	17	Turkey	28	South Africa
10	Serbia	18	Czech Republic	29	Mexico
11	India	19	Costa Rica	30	Venezuela

Listed Alphabetically

Argentina, 21. 205 N Michigan Ave
☎ 819-2610

Australia, 26. 123 N Wacker Dr
☎ 541-0414

Austria, 13. 400 N Michigan Ave
☎ 222-1515

Belgium, 16. 333 N Michigan Ave
☎ 263-6624

Brazil, 12. 401 N Michigan Ave
☎ 464-0244

Canada, 22. 180 N Stetson Ave
☎ 616-1860

China, 2 100 W Erie St
☎ 803-0095

Costa Rica, 19. 203 N Wabash Ave
☎ 263-2772

Croatia, 3. 737 N Michigan Ave
☎ 482-9902

Czech Rrepublic, 18.
225 N Michigan Ave ☎ 540-1367

Denmark, 7. 211 E Ontario St
☎ 787-8780

Egypt, 14. 500 N Michigan Ave
☎ 828-9162

France, 21. 205 N Michigan Ave
☎ 327-5200

Germany, 6. 676 N Michigan Ave
☎ 202-0480

Great Britian, 13. 400 N Michigan Ave
☎ 970-3800

Greece, 20. 151 N Michigan Ave
☎ 228-9516

Haiti, 27. 220 S State St ☎ 922-4004

India, 11. 455 N City Front Plaza Dr
☎ 595-0405

Indonesia, 24. 211 W Wacker Dr
☎ 920-1880

Ireland, 13. 400 N Michigan Ave
☎ 337-1868

Israel, 23. 111 E Wacker Dr
☎ 297-4800

Italy, 14. 500 N Michigan Ave
☎ 467-1550

Japan, 3. 737 N Michigan Ave
☎ 280-2400

Korea, 11. 455 N Cityfront Plaza Dr
☎ 822-0017

Lithuania, 9. 211 E Ontario St
☎ 397-0382

Mexico, 29. 204 S Ashland Dr
☎ 855-1380

Netherlands, 15. 303 E Wacker Dr
☎ 856-0110

Pakistan, 16. 333 N Michigan Ave
☎ 781-1831

Philippines, 25. 30 N Michigan Ave
☎ 332-6458

Poland, 1. 1530 N Lake Shore Dr
☎ 337-8166

Serbia, 10. 201 E Ohio St
☎ 670-6707

South Africa, 28. 200 S Michigan Ave
☎ 939-7929

Spain, 20. 180 N Michigan Ave
☎ 782-4588

Switzerland, 3. 737 N Michigan Ave
☎ 915-0061

Thailand, 4. 700 N Rush St
☎ 664-3129

Turkey, 17. 360 N Michigan Ave
☎ 701-1262

Ukraine, 5. 10 E Huron St
☎ 642-4388

Venezuela, 30. 20 N Wacker Dr
☎ 236-9655

Listed by Site Number

1 Gerber/Hart Library
2 Edgewater
3 Budlong Woods
4 Albany Park
5 Northeast Illinois University
6 Mayfair
7 Independence
8 Sulzer Regional
9 Bezazian
10 Uptown
11 John Merlo
12 Lincoln Belmont
13 Lincoln Park
14 Bucktown-Wicker Park
15 Logan Square
16 Humboldt Park
17 Legler
18 Midwest
19 Eckhart Park
20 Near North
21 Chicago History Museum
22 Newberry Library
23 Moody Bible Institute
24 Instituto Cervantes
25 Pritzker Military Library
26 Goethe-Institut Chicago
27 Cook County Law Library
28 Donors Forum of Chicago
29 Burnham Library
30 Harrington Institute of Interior Design
31 DePaul University Law Library
32 Robert Morris College
33 Chinatown
34 Asher Library
35 Harold Washington Library Center
36 Chicago Board of Trade
37 Chicago-Kent College of Law
38 Mabel Manning
39 Roosevelt
40 Rudy Lozano
41 Legler
42 Douglass
43 Marshall Square
44 Toman
45 Archer Heights
46 Brighton Park
47 West Lawn
48 Chicago Lawn
49 Gage Park
50 Lithuanian Research and Studies Center
51 Back of the Yards
52 Sherman Park
53 Canaryville
54 McKinley Park
55 Richard J. Daley
56 Chicago Bee
57 Martin Luther King, Jr
58 Hall
59 Blackstone
60 John Crerar Science Library
61 Kelly
62 West Englewood
63 Woodson Regional
64 Coleman
65 South Shore

Listed Alphabetically

PUBLIC

Albany Park, 4. 5150 N Kimball Ave ☎ 744-1933

Archer Heights, 45. 5055 S Archer Ave ☎ 747-9241

Back of the Yards, 51. 4650 S Damen Ave ☎ 747-8367

Bezazian, 9. 1226 W Ainslie St ☎ 744-0019

Blackstone, 59. 4904 S Lake Park Ave ☎ 747-0511

Brighton Park, 46. 4314 S Archer Ave ☎ 747-0666

Bucktown-Wicker Park, 14. 1701 N Milwaukee Ave ☎ 744-6022

Budlong Woods, 3. 5630 N Lincoln Ave ☎ 742-9590

Canaryville, 53. 642 W 43rd St ☎ 747-0644

Chicago Bee, 56. 3647 S State St ☎ 747-6872

Chicago Lawn, 48. 6120 S Kedzie Ave ☎ 747-0639

Chinatown, 33. 2353 S Wentworth Ave ☎ 747-8013

Coleman, 64. 731 E 63rd St ☎ 747-7760

Douglass, 42. 3353 W 13th St ☎ 747-3725

Eckhart Park, 19. 1371 W Chicago Ave ☎ 746-6069

Edgewater, 2. 1210 W Elmdale Ave ☎ 744-0718

Gage Park, 49. 2807 W 55th St ☎ 747-0032

Hall, 58. 4801 S Michigan Ave ☎ 747-2541

Harold Washington Library Center, 35. 400 S State St ☎ 747-4300

Humboldt Park, 16. 1605 N Troy St. ☎ 744-2244

Independence, 7. 3548 W Irving Park Rd ☎ 744-0900

John Merlo, 11. 644 W Belmont Ave ☎ 744-1139

Kelly, 61. 6151 S Normal Blvd ☎ 747-8418

Legler, 41. 115 S Pulaski Rd ☎ 746-7730

Listed Alphabetically

Lincoln Belmont, 12.
1659 W Melrose St
☎ 744-0166

Lincoln Park, 13.
1150 W. Fullerton Ave ☎ 744-1926

Logan Square, 15.
3030 W Fullerton ☎ 744-5295

Mabel Manning, 38.
6 S Hoyne Ave ☎ 746-6800

Marshall Square, 43.
2724 W Cermak Rd ☎ 747-0061

Martin Luther King, Jr, 57.
3436 S King Dr ☎ 747-7543

Mayfair, 6.
4400 W Lawrence Ave ☎ 744-1254

McKinley Park, 54.
1915 W 35th St ☎ 747-6082

Midwest, 18.
2335 W Chicago Ave ☎ 744-7788

Near North, 20.
310 W Division St ☎ 744-0991

North Pulaski, 17.
4300 W North Ave ☎ 744-9573

Richard J. Daley, 55.
3400 S Halsted St ☎ 747-8990

Roosevelt, 39.
1101 W Taylor St ☎ 746-5656

Rudy Lozano, 40.
1805 S Loomis St ☎ 746-4329

Sherman Park, 52.
5440 S Racine Ave ☎ 747-0477

South Shore, 65.
2505 E 73rd St ☎ 747-5281

Sulzer Regional, 8.
4455 N Lincoln Ave ☎ 744-7616

Toman, 44.
2708 S Pulaski Rd ☎ 745-1660

Uptown, 10.
929 W Buena Ave
☎ 744-8400

West Englewood, 62.
1745 W 63rd St ☎ 747-3481

West Lawn, 47.
4020 W 63rd St ☎ 747-7381

Woodson Regional, 63.
9525 S. Halsted St ☎ 747-6900

PROFESSIONAL

**Asher Library at Spertus Institute
of Jewish Studies, 34.**
610 S Michigan Ave ☎ 322-1712

**Burnham Library at
Art Institute of Chicago, 29.**
111 S Michigan Ave ☎ 443-3666

**Chicago Board of Trade
Reading Room, 36.**
141 W Jackson Blvd ☎ 435-3552

Chicago History Museum, 21.
1601 N. Clark St ☎ 642-4600

**Chicago-Kent College of
Law Library, 37.**
565 W Adams St
☎ 905-5600

Cook County Law Library, 27.
50 W Washington Blvd ☎ 603-5423

DePaul University Law Library, 31.
25 E Jackson Blvd ☎ 362-8121

Donors Forum of Chicago, 28.
208 S LaSalle St ☎ 578-0090

**Gerber/Hart Gay and
Lesbian Library, 1.**
1127 W Granville Ave ☎ 773/381-8030

Goethe-Institut Chicago, 26.
150 N Michigan Ave ☎ 263-0472

**Harrington Institute of
Interior Design Library, 30.**
200 W Madison St ☎ 939-4975

Instituto Cervantes, 24.
31 W Ohio Ave ☎ 335-1996

John Crerar Science Library, 60.
5730 S Ellis Ave ☎ 773/702-7715

**Lithuanian Research and
Studies Center, 50.**
5620 S Claremont Ave
☎ 773/434-4545

Moody Bible Institute Library, 23.
860 N LaSalle St ☎ 329-4136

Newberry Library, 22.
60 W Walton St ☎ 943-9090

**Northeastern Illinois
University Library, 5.**
5500 N St. Louis Ave ☎ 773/442-4400

Pritzker Military Library, 25.
247 E Ontario ☎ 587-0234

Robert Morris College, 32.
401 S State St ☎ 935-4812

Listed by Site Number

1. Loyola University
2. Northeastern Illinois University
3. North Park University
4. Truman College
5. Wright College
6. Chicago National College of Naprapathy
7. Kendall College
8. DePaul University
9. Cooking and Hospitality Institute of Chicago
10. Moody Bible Institute
11. Loyola University
12. Northwestern University
13. University of Chicago–GSB
14. Illinois Institute of Art
15. Chicago School of Professional Psychology
16. Harold Washington College
17. Adler School of Professional Psychology
18. Cortiva Institute–Chicago School of Massage Therapy

19. School of the Art Institute of Chicago
20. National-Louis University
21. John Marshall Law School
22. Robert Morris College
23. American Academy of Art
24. DePaul University
25. Lake Forest Graduate School of Management
26. Roosevelt University
27. Columbia College
28. Spertus Institute of Jewish Studies
29. East-West University
30. University of Illinois at Chicago
31. Chicago–Kent College of Law
32. Flashpoint Academy
33. Harrington College of Design
34. Malcolm X College
35. Rush University Chicago
36. West Side Technical Institute

37. Illinois Institute of Technology
38. Illinois College of Optometry
39. Lutheran School of Theology
40. McCormick Theological Seminary
41. Chicago Theological Seminary
42. University of Chicago
43. Chicago State University
44. Olive-Harvey College
45. Kennedy-King College
46. Richard J Daley College

Listed Alphabetically

Adler School of Professional Psychology, 17.
65 E Wacker Pl ☎ 201-5900

American Academy of Art, 23.
332 S Michigan Ave ☎ 461-0600

Chicago-Kent College of Law, 31.
565 W Adams St ☎ 906-5000

Chicago National College of Naprapathy, 6. 3330 N Milwaukee Ave ☎ 773/282-2686

Cortiva Institute-Chicago School of Massage Therapy, 18.
17 N State St #500 ☎ 753-7900

Chicago School of Professional Psychology, 15.
325 N Wells ☎ 329-6600

Chicago State University, 43.
9501 S Martin Luther King Dr ☎ 773/995-2000

Chicago Theological Seminary, 41.
5757 S University Ave ☎ 773/752-5757

Columbia College, 27.
600 S Michigan Ave ☎ 663-1600

Cooking and Hospitality Institute of Chicago, 9.
361 W Chestnut St ☎ 888/295-7222

DePaul University, Loop Campus, 24.
1 E Jackson Blvd ☎ 362-8000

DePaul University, 8.
2352 N Clifton Ave ☎ 773/325-7310

East-West University, 29.
816 S Michigan Ave ☎ 939-0111

Flashpoint Academy, 32.
28 N Clark St ☎ 332-0707

Harold Washington College, 16.
30 E Lake St ☎ 553-5600

Harrington College of Design, 33.
200 W Madison St ☎ 866/590-4423

Illinois College of Optometry, 38.
3241 S Michigan Ave ☎ 949-7000

Illinois Institute of Art, 14.
350 N Orleans St ☎ 800/351-3450

Illinois Institute of Technology, 37.
3300 S Federal St ☎ 567-3000

John Marshall Law School, 21.
315 S Plymouth Ct ☎ 427-2737

Kendall College, 7.
900 N Branch St ☎ 866/667-3344

Kennedy-King College, 45.
6301 S Halsted St ☎ 773/602-5000

Lake Forest Graduate School of Management, 25.
230 S LaSalle St ☎ 435-5330

Loyola Unversity, 1.
6525 N Sheridan Ave
☎ 773/274-3000

Loyola Unversity, 11.
Water Tower Campus
820 N Michigan Ave
☎ 915-6000

Lutheran School of Theology, 39.
1100 E 55th St ☎ 773/753-0700

Malcolm X College, 34.
1900 W Van Buren Ave ☎ 850-7000

McCormick Theological Seminary, 40. 5460 S University Ave
☎ 773/947-6300

Moody Bible Institute, 10.
820 N LaSalle St ☎ 644-7554

National-Louis University, 20.
122 S Michigan Ave
☎ 888-NLU-TODAY

North Park University, 3.
3225 W Foster Ave ☎ 773/244-6200

Northeastern Illinois University, 2.
5500 N St. Louis Ave ☎ 773/583-4050

Northwestern University, 12.
710 N Lake Shore Dr ☎ 503-8649

Olive-Harvey College, 44.
10001 S Woodlawn Ave
☎ 773/291-6100

Richard J Daley College, 46.
7500 S Pulaski Rd ☎ 773/838-7500

Robert Morris College, 22.
401 S State St ☎ 935-6800

Roosevelt University, 26.
430 S Michigan Ave ☎ 341-3500

Rush University Chicago, 35.
600 S Paulina St ☎ 942-5000

School of the Art Institute of Chicago, 19.
37 S Wabash Ave ☎ 899-5100

Spertus Institute of Jewish Studies, 28. 610 S Michigan Ave ☎ 922-9012

Truman College, 4.
1145 W Wilson Ave ☎ 773/878-1700

University of Chicago, 42.
5801 S Ellis Ave ☎ 773/702-1234

University of Chicago-GSB, 13.
450 N City Front Plaza Dr ☎ 464-8777

University of Illinois at Chicago, 30.
1200 W Harrison St ☎ 996-7000

West Side Technical Institute, 36.
2800 S Western Ave ☎ 773/843-4500

Wright College, 5.
4300 N Narragansett Ave
☎ 773/777-7900

Listed by Site Number

1 Ratner Athletic Center
2 Court Theatre
3 Cochrane-Woods Art Center
4 Smart Museum
5 Pierce Hall
6 Henry Crown Field House
7 Max Palevsky Residential Commons
8 Research Institutes
9 Regenstein Library
10 Ronald McDonald House
11 Comer Children's Hospital
12 Crerar Library
13 Kersten Physics Teaching Center
14 Snell-Hitchcock Halls
15 Quadrangle Club
16 Reynolds Club/University Theater
17 Mandel Hall

18 Jones Laboratory
19 Kent Chemical Laboratory
20 Ryerson Physical Laboratory
21 Hinds Laboratory
22 Cummings Life Science Center
23 Kovler Viral Oncology Laboratories
24 Bernard Mitchell Hospital/Chicago Lying-in Hospital
25 University Hospitals
26 Administration Building
27 Cobb Hall
28 Swift Hall
29 Bond Chapel
30 Rosenwald Hall
31 Oriental Institute
32 Robie House
33 International House
34 Breckenridge House
35 Ida Noyes Hall

36 Graduate School of Business
37 Rockefeller Memorial Chapel
38 Social Science Research
39 Stuart Hall
40 Harper Memorial Library/College Admissions
41 Classics Building
42 Midway Studios
43 Social Service Administration
44 Burton-Judson Courts
45 Laird Bell Law Quadrangle/D'Angelo Law Library
46 1155 Building
47 Harris School
48 Midway Skating Rink
49 David Logan Arts Center (opens 2011)
50 New Graduate Residence Hall
51 Center for Research Libraries

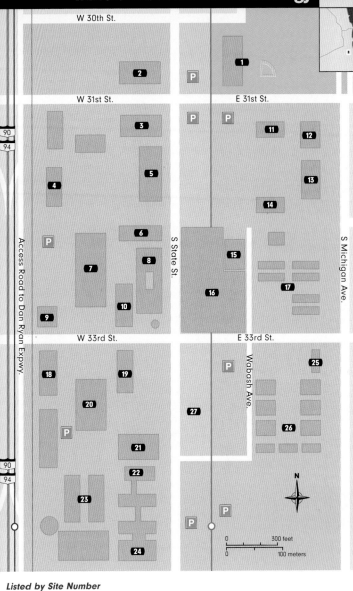

Listed by Site Number

1 Keating Sports Ctr
2 Stuart
3 Life Sciences
4 VanderCook College of Music
5 Eng 1 Building
6 Alumni Memorial Hall
7 Hermann Union
8 Perlstein Hall
9 Machinery Hall
10 Wishnick
11 Bailey Hall Apts
12 Cunningham Hall Apts
13 Gunsaulus Hall Apts
14 Carman Hall Apts
15 Commons Building
16 McCormick Tribune Campus Center
17 Residence Halls/ McCormick Student Village
18 Main Building
19 Siegel
20 Galvin Library
21 Crown Hall
22 World Learning Center
23 IITRI Complex
24 IIT Tower
25 Farr Hall
26 Fraternity Complex
27 State Street Village

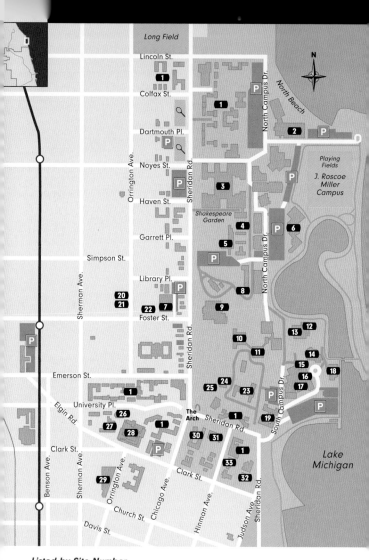

Listed by Site Number

1 Student Residences	**11** University Library	**22** Hillel Foundation
2 Crown Sports Pavilion	**12** Norris University Ctr	**23** Kresge Centennial Hall
3 McCormick Technological Institute	**13** McCormick Auditorium	**24** University Hall
4 Dearborn Observatory	**14** Pick-Staiger Concert Hall	**25** The Rock
5 Garret Evangelical Theological Seminary	**15** Block Museum	**26** Lutkin Hall
6 Allen Center	**16** Theatre and Interpretation Ctr	**27** Music Administration
7 Blomquist Recreation Center	**17** Marjorie Ward Marshall Dance Ctr	**28** Rebecca Crown Center
8 Cresap Laboratory	**18** Regenstein Hall of Music	**29** Orrington Hotel
9 Jacobs Center	**19** Fisk Hall	**30** Alice Millar Chapel
10 Deering Library	**20** Chabad House	**31** Levere Temple
	21 Canterbury House	**32** John Evans Alumni Center
		33 University Police

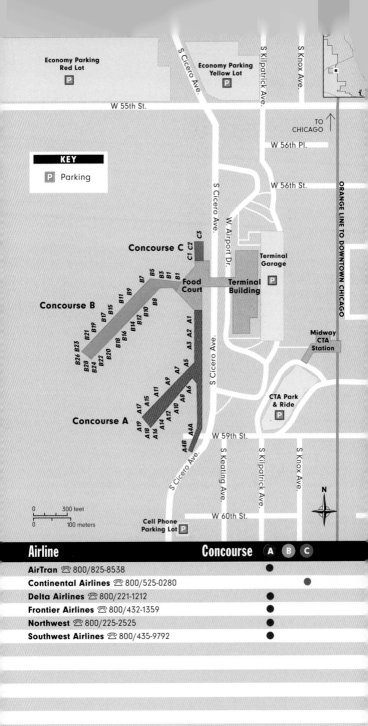

Economy Parking Red Lot P

S Cicero Ave.

Economy Parking Yellow Lot P

S Kilpatrick Ave.

S Knox Ave.

W 55th St.

TO CHICAGO

W 56th Pl.

ORANGE LINE TO DOWNTOWN CHICAGO

W 56th St.

KEY
P Parking

S Cicero Ave.

W. Airport Dr.

Concourse C C1 C2 C3

Terminal Garage P

B5 B3 B1
B7 B1
B9

Food Court

Terminal Building

Concourse B
B11
B15 B13
B17
B19 B10
B21 B12 B8
B18 B14
B22 B16
B28 B20
B26 B24
B23

A2 A1
A3
A5 A4
A7
A9
A11
A17 A8
A15 A10
A12
A18 A14
A16
A19 A6

S Cicero Ave.

Midway CTA Station

CTA Park & Ride P

Concourse A

A4A
A4B

W 59th St.

S Keating Ave.

S Kilpatrick Ave.

S Knox Ave.

N

S Cicero Ave.

| 0 | 300 feet |
| 0 | 100 meters |

Cell Phone Parking Lot P

W 60th St.

Airline	Concourse	A	B	C
AirTran ☎ 800/825-8538		●		
Continental Airlines ☎ 800/525-0280				●
Delta Airlines ☎ 800/221-1212		●		
Frontier Airlines ☎ 800/432-1359		●		
Northwest ☎ 800/225-2525		●		
Southwest Airlines ☎ 800/435-9792		●		

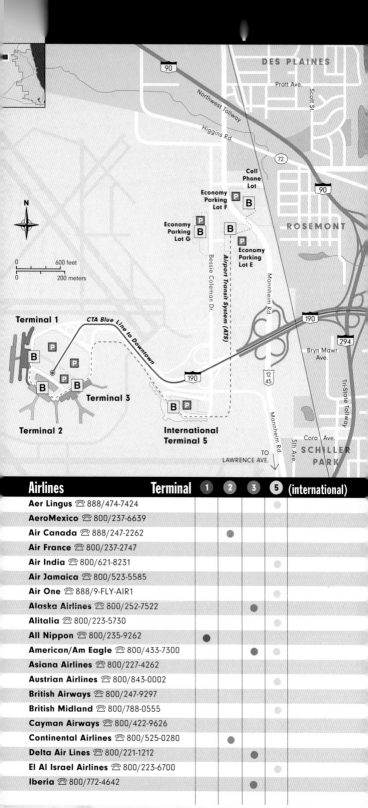

DES PLAINES

Pratt Ave.
Scott St.

90

Northwest Tollway

Higgins Rd.

72

90

Cell
Phone
Lot

Economy
Parking
Lot F

P

B

ROSEMONT

Economy
Parking
Lot G

P

B

B

P

B

Economy
Parking
Lot E

190

294

Bryn Mawr
Ave.

N

0   600 feet
0   200 meters

Bessie Coleman Dr.

Airport Transit System (ATS)

Mannheim Rd.

190

12
45

Tri-State Tollway

Terminal 1

CTA Blue Line to Downtown

P

B

P

B

P

B

Terminal 3

B

P

190

Mannheim Rd.

5th Ave.

Cora Ave.

**SCHILLER
PARK**

Terminal 2

**International
Terminal 5**

TO
LAWRENCE AVE.

Airlines Terminal	1	2	3	5 (international)
Aer Lingus ☎ 888/474-7424				●
AeroMexico ☎ 800/237-6639				
Air Canada ☎ 888/247-2262		●		
Air France ☎ 800/237-2747				
Air India ☎ 800/621-8231				●
Air Jamaica ☎ 800/523-5585				
Air One ☎ 888/9-FLY-AIR1				
Alaska Airlines ☎ 800/252-7522			●	
Alitalia ☎ 800/223-5730				●
All Nippon ☎ 800/235-9262	●			
American/Am Eagle ☎ 800/433-7300			●	●
Asiana Airlines ☎ 800/227-4262				
Austrian Airlines ☎ 800/843-0002				●
British Airways ☎ 800/247-9297				
British Midland ☎ 800/788-0555				●
Cayman Airways ☎ 800/422-9626				
Continental Airlines ☎ 800/525-0280		●		
Delta Air Lines ☎ 800/221-1212			●	
El Al Israel Airlines ☎ 800/223-6700				●
Iberia ☎ 800/772-4642			●	

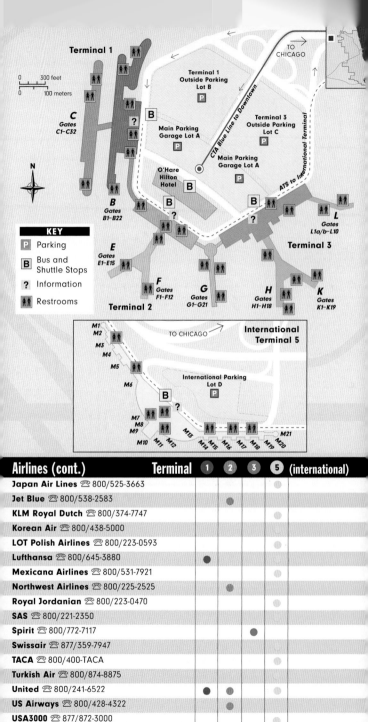

Airlines (cont.)	Terminal	1	2	3	5 (international)
Japan Air Lines ☏ 800/525-3663					●
Jet Blue ☏ 800/538-2583			●		
KLM Royal Dutch ☏ 800/374-7747					●
Korean Air ☏ 800/438-5000					●
LOT Polish Airlines ☏ 800/223-0593					●
Lufthansa ☏ 800/645-3880		●			
Mexicana Airlines ☏ 800/531-7921					●
Northwest Airlines ☏ 800/225-2525			●		
Royal Jordanian ☏ 800/223-0470					●
SAS ☏ 800/221-2350					
Spirit ☏ 800/772-7117				●	
Swissair ☏ 877/359-7947					
TACA ☏ 800/400-TACA					●
Turkish Air ☏ 800/874-8875					
United ☏ 800/241-6522		●	●		●
US Airways ☏ 800/428-4322			●		
USA3000 ☏ 877/872-3000					●
Virgin Atlantic ☏ 800/821-5438					

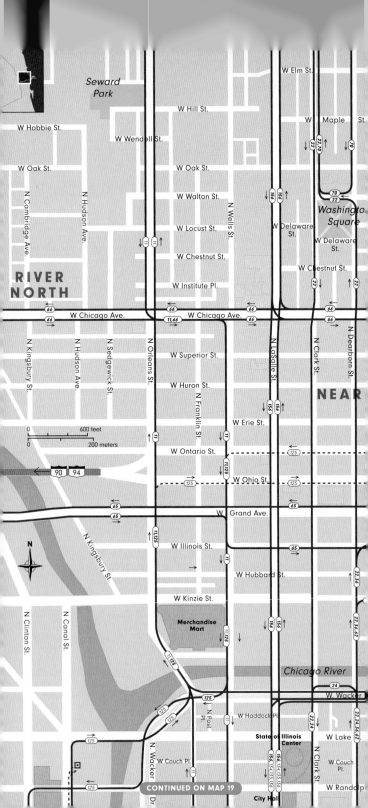

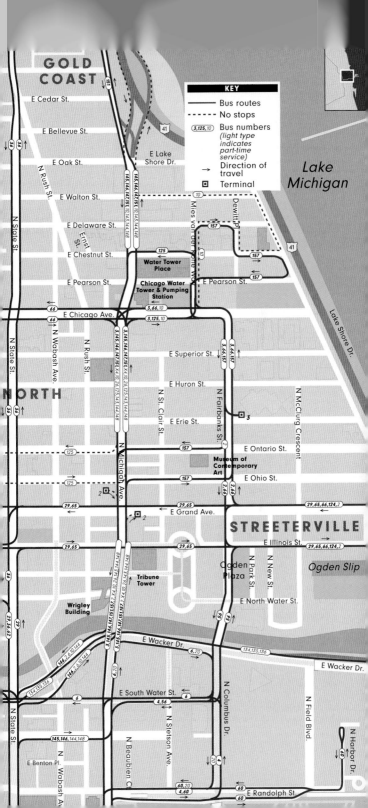

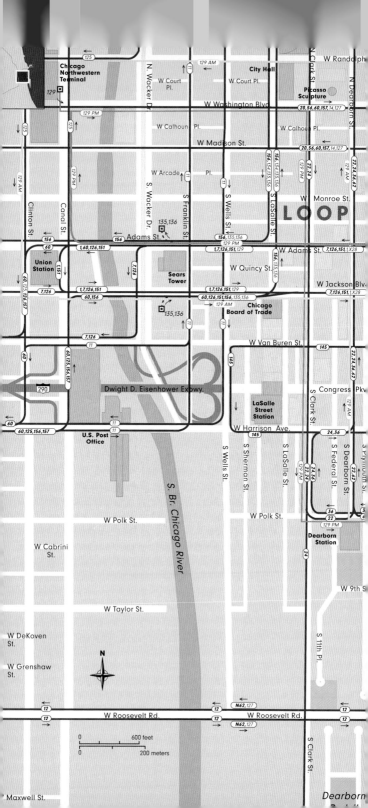

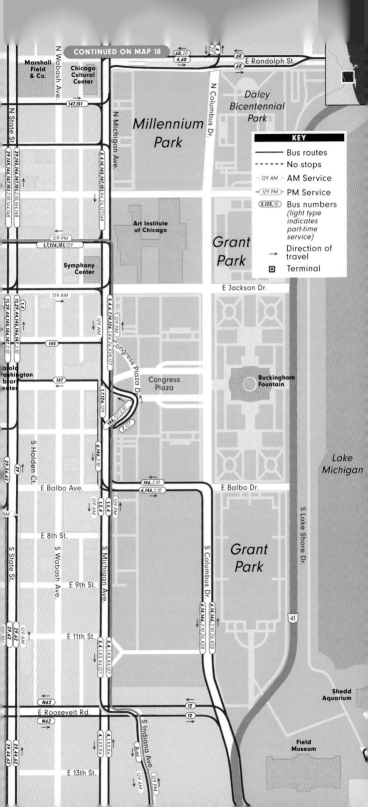

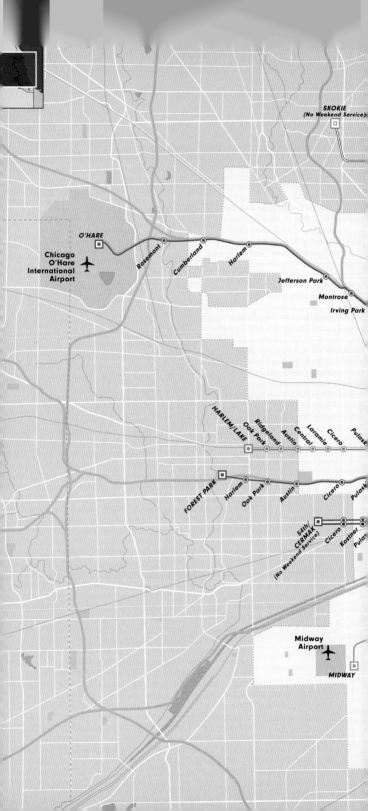

■ LINDEN
● Central
● Noyes
● Foster
● Davis
● Dempster
● Main
● South Blvd
■ HOWARD
□ Jarvis
● Morse
● Loyola
● Granville
● Thorndale
● Bryn Mawr
● Berwyn
● Argyle
● Lawrence
● Wilson
● Sheridan
● Addison
● Belmont
● Wellington
● Diversey
● Fullerton
● Armitage
● North/Clybourn

Western
Francisco
Rockwell
Kedzie
ALL
Damen

Montrose
Irving Park
Addison
Addison
Paulina
Southport
Belmont
Logan Sq
California
Western
Damen
Division
Chicago
Grand
Clinton
Ashland
Clinton

Conservatory/
California/
Kedzie

Kedzie/
Homan
Western
Medical Ctr
Polk
Racine
UIC/
Halsted
Roosevelt

18th
Cermak/Chinatown
Halsted

Central Park
Kedzie
California
Damen
Western

Ashland
35th/Archer
Sox/35th
35th/Bronzeville/IIT
Indiana
43rd
47th
47th
51st
Garfield
Garfield
ML King Dr
(Inbound only)

Kedzie
Western
Pulaski

ASHLAND/63rd
Halsted
63rd
E 63rd/
COTTAGE GROVE
69th
79th
87th
95/DAN RYAN

SEE MAPS 21 & 22
FOR DETAILED VIEW OF
DOWNTOWN CTA

Lake Michigan

KEY

— **Red Line**
  Howard–Dan Ryan
— **Brown Line**
  Ravenswood
— **Purple Line**
  *Evanston Shuttle &
  Express*
═ **Yellow Line**
  Skokie Swift
— **Blue Line**
  *O'Hare–Forest Park–
  Cermak*
— **Green Line**
  *Lake–Ashland–
  E 63rd*
— **Orange Line**
  Midway
— **Pink Line**
  54th & Cermak

STATIONS
■ Terminal
■ Free transfer

—— Metra lines

0   1   2 miles
0   1   2 km

N

KEY

▣ Free transfer

▦ Metra lines

Sedgwick

OLD TOWN

N Cleveland St.
N Hudson St.
N Sedgwick St.
N Orleans St.
N Park St.
N Wieland St.
N Wells St.

W Schiller St.

W Sullivan St.

W Evergreen St.

W Goethe St.

W Goethe St.

W Scott St.

N LaSalle St.
N Clark St.
N Dearborn St.
N Parkway St.

W Division St.

W Division St.

Clark/ Division

W Elm St.

Seward Park

W Hill St.

W Maple St.

W Wendell St.

W Oak St.

W Walton St.

N Hudson Ave.

N Wells St.

Washington Square

W Delaware St.

W Delaware St.

W Locust St.

W Chestnut St.

W Chestnut St.

RIVER NORTH

W Institute Pl.

Chicago

N State St.

Chicago

W Chicago Ave.

W Chicago Ave.

N Hudson Ave.
N Sedgwick St.
N Orleans St.
N Franklin St.

W Superior St.

W Huron St.

N LaSalle St.
N Clark St.
N Dearborn St.
N State St.

NEAR NORTH

W Erie St.

W Ontario St.

N

W Ohio St.

0   600 feet
0   200 meters

Grand

N Kingsbury St.

W Grand Ave.

CONTINUED ON MAP 22

W Illinois St.

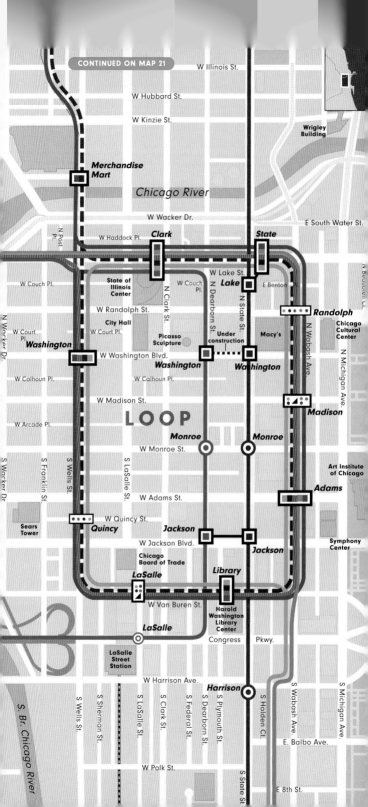

CONTINUED ON MAP 21

W Illinois St.

W Hubbard St.

W Kinzie St.

Wrigley
Building

Merchandise
Mart

Chicago River

W Wacker Dr.

E South Water St.

W Haddock Pl.

Clark

State

N Post
Pl.

W Couch Pl.

State of
Illinois
Center

N Clark St.

W Couch
Pl.

N Dearborn St.

W Lake St.

N State St.

Lake

E Benton

N Wabash Ave.

Randolph

Chicago
Cultural
Center

W Randolph St.

City Hall

W Court Pl.

W Court Pl.

Picasso
Sculpture

Under
construction

Macy's

N Michigan Ave.

W Couch Pl.

W Wacker Dr

S Wacker Dr

N Wacker Dr

Washington

Washington

Washington

W Washington Blvd.

W Calhoun Pl.

W Calhoun Pl.

Madison

W Madison St.

W Arcade Pl.

LOOP

Monroe

Monroe

W Monroe St.

S Franklin St.

S Wells St.

S LaSalle St.

Art Institute
of Chicago

W Adams St.

Adams

Quincy

W Quincy St.

Sears
Tower

Jackson

Jackson

W Jackson Blvd.

Chicago
Board of
Trade

Symphony
Center

LaSalle

Library

W Van Buren St.

Harold
Washington
Library
Center

LaSalle

Congress   Pkwy.

LaSalle
Street
Station

W Harrison Ave.

Harrison

S Wells St.

S Sherman St.

S LaSalle St.

S Clark St.

S Federal St.

S Dearborn St.

S Plymouth St.

S State St.

S Holden Ct.

S Wabash Ave.

S Michigan Ave.

E. Balbo Ave.

S. Br. Chicago River

W Polk St.

E 8th St.

TO KENOSHA, WI

Ⓘ *Winthrop Harbor*

Ⓘ *Zion*

UNION PACIFIC NORTH LINE

Ⓗ *Waukegan*

Ⓖ *N Chicago*

Ⓖ *Great Lakes*

MILWAUKEE DISTRICT NORTH LINE

Ⓗ
Libertyville

Ⓖ *Lake Bluff*

Lake Michigan

Ⓕ *Lake Forest*

Ⓕ *Lake Forest*

Ⓕ *Fort Sheridan*

Ⓖ *Vernon Hills*

Ⓖ *Prairie View*

Ⓕ *Highwood*

Ⓕ *Buffalo Grove*

Deerfield **Ⓔ**

Ⓕ *Highland Park*

Ⓔ *Ravinia*
Ravinia Park
Ⓔ *Braeside*

Lake Cook Rd **Ⓔ**

Ⓕ *Wheeling*

Northbrook **Ⓔ**

Ⓓ *Glencoe*

Ⓓ *Hubbard Woods*

Ⓓ *Winnetka*

Ⓓ *Indian Hill*

Ⓒ
Arlington Heights

Ⓕ *Prospect Heights*

Ⓓ *Kenilworth*

Ⓒ *Wilmette*

Ⓓ *Mt Prospect*

Ⓓ
Cumberland

The Glen/ N Glenview **Ⓓ**
Ⓓ *Glenview*

Golf **Ⓓ**

Ⓒ *Central St/Evanston*

Ⓒ *Des Plaines*

Morton Grove **Ⓒ**

Ⓒ *Davis St/Evanston*

Ⓒ *Main St/Evanston*

Ⓒ *Dee Road*

Park Ridge **Ⓒ**

Ⓒ *Edison Park*

Chicago O'Hare International Airport

Ⓓ *O'Hare Transfer*

Norwood Park **Ⓒ**

Edgebrook **Ⓒ**

Ⓑ *Rogers Park*

Wood Dale

Ⓓ *Bensenville*

Gladstone Park **Ⓑ**
Jefferson Park **Ⓑ**
Mayfair **Ⓑ**

Ⓑ *Forest Glen*

Ⓑ *Ravenswood*

Irving Park **Ⓑ**

CONTINUED ON MAP 24

KEY

▬▬▬ Metra commuter lines

STATIONS

Ⓐ Terminal
Ⓐ Full service
Ⓑ Partial service
Ⓗ Under construction
(letters indicate fare zone)

——— CTA lines

N

0 ——————— 2 miles
0 ——————— 2 km

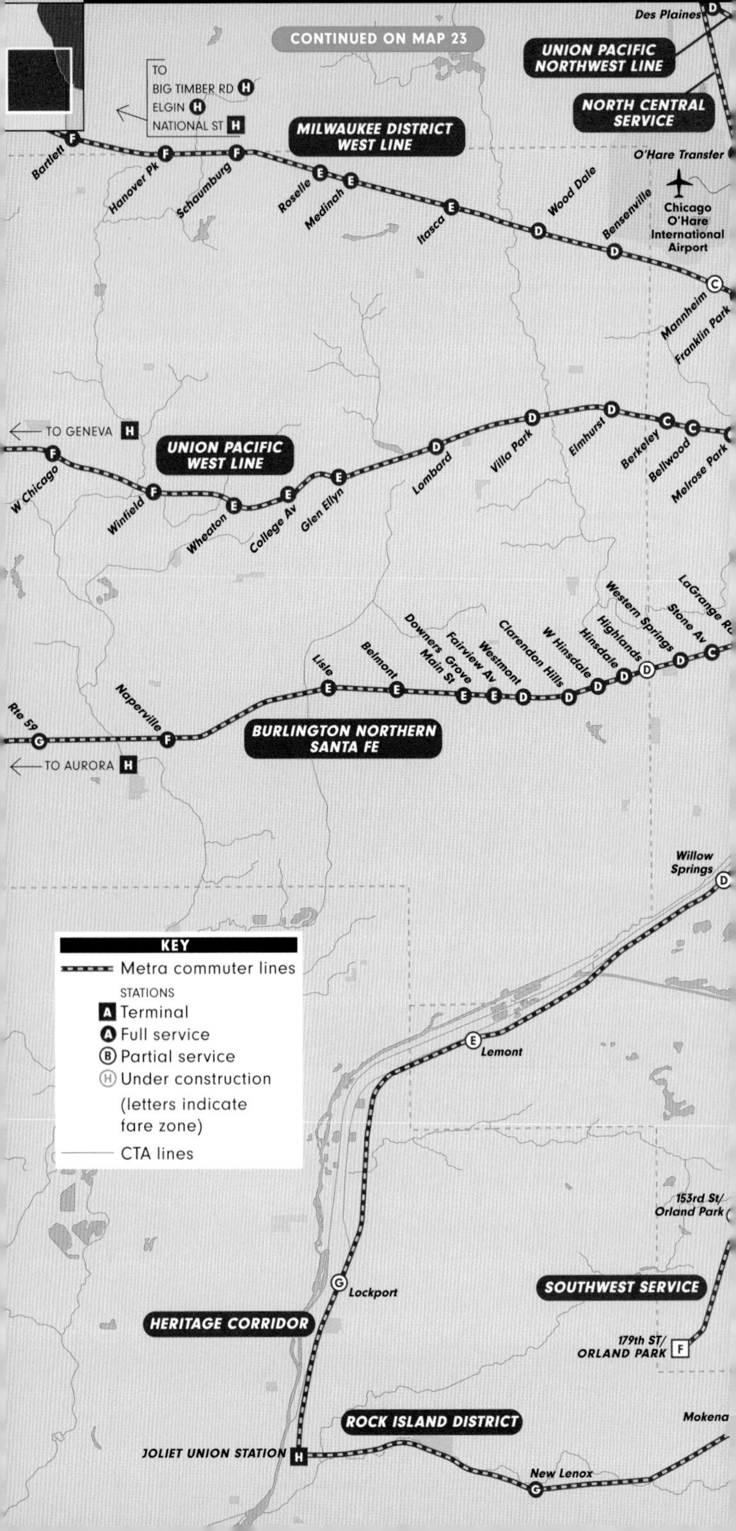

MAP 24 **Metra/ Western & Southern Suburbs**

Des Plaines **D**

CONTINUED ON MAP 23

**UNION PACIFIC
NORTHWEST LINE**

TO
BIG TIMBER RD **H**
ELGIN **H**
NATIONAL ST **H**

**NORTH CENTRAL
SERVICE**

**MILWAUKEE DISTRICT
WEST LINE**

O'Hare Transfer

Bartlett **F**
Hanover Pk **F**
Schaumburg **F**
Roselle **E**
Medinah **E**
Itasca **E**
Wood Dale **D**
Bensenville **D**

Chicago
O'Hare
International
Airport

Mannheim **C**
Franklin Park

TO GENEVA **H**

**UNION PACIFIC
WEST LINE**

W Chicago **F**
Winfield **F**
Wheaton **E**
College Av **E**
Glen Ellyn **E**
Lombard **D**
Villa Park **D**
Elmhurst **D**
Berkeley **C**
Bellwood **C**
Melrose Park **C**

LaGrange Rd **C**
Stone Av **C**
Western Springs
Highlands **D**
Hinsdale **D**
W Hinsdale **D**
Clarendon Hills **D**
Westmont **D**
Fairview Av
Main St
Downers Grove
Belmont **E**
Lisle **E**
Naperville **F**
Rte 59 **C**

TO AURORA **H**

**BURLINGTON NORTHERN
SANTA FE**

Willow
Springs **D**

KEY
▭▭▭ Metra commuter lines
STATIONS
A Terminal
A Full service
B Partial service
H Under construction
(letters indicate
fare zone)
──── CTA lines

Lemont **E**

153rd St/
Orland Park

Lockport **G**

SOUTHWEST SERVICE

HERITAGE CORRIDOR

179th St/
ORLAND PARK F

ROCK ISLAND DISTRICT

Mokena

JOLIET UNION STATION **H**

New Lenox **G**

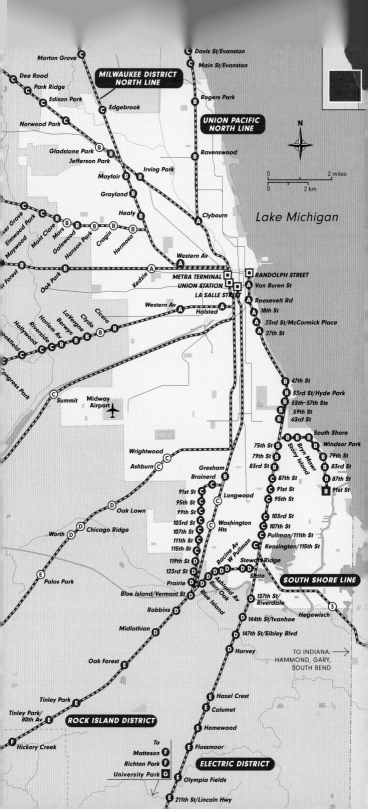

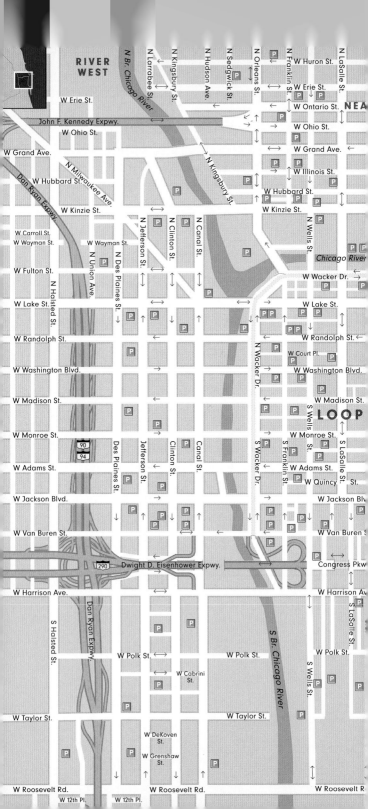

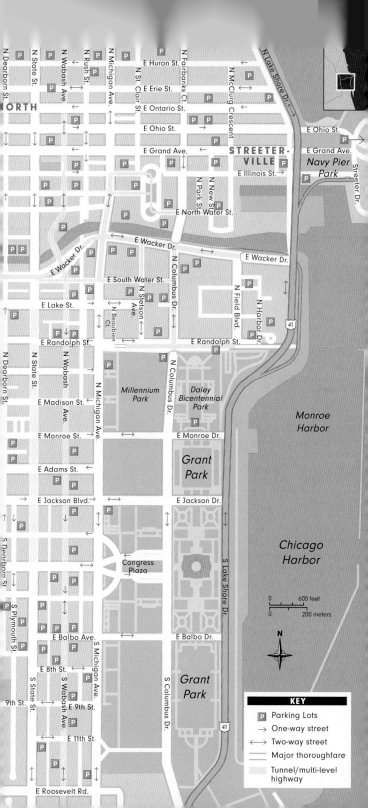

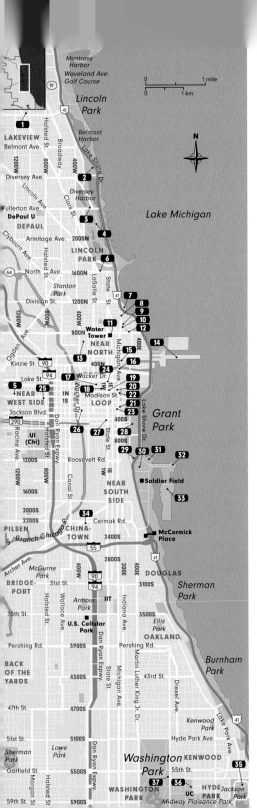

Listed by
Site Number

1 Wrigley Field
2 Lincoln Park
3 Peggy Notebaert Nature Museum
4 Lincoln Park Zoo
5 United Center
6 Chicago History Museum
7 Oak Street Beach
8 Magnificent Mile
9 John Hancock Observatory
10 Water Tower Place
11 Chicago Water Tower and Pumping Station
12 Museum of Contemporary Art
13 River North Gallery District
14 Chicago Children's Museum
14 Navy Pier
15 Tribune Tower
16 Michigan Avenue Bridge
17 State of Illinois Center
18 *Untitled,* Picasso
19 Marshall Field & Co
20 Chicago Cultural Center
21 Millenium Park
22 Art Institute of Chicago
23 Symphony Center
24 Chicago Theater
25 Greektown
26 Sears Tower
27 Harold Washington Library Center
28 Grant Park
29 Skyline View
30 Field Museum of Natural Museum
31 John G Shedd Aquarium
32 Adler Planetarium
33 Charter One Pavilion
34 Chinatown
35 Museum of Science and Industry
36 University of Chicago
37 DuSable Museum of African American History

Listed Alphabetically

Adler Planetarium, 32.
1300 S Lake Shore Dr ☎ 922-7827

Art Institute of Chicago, 22.
111 S Michigan Ave ☎ 443-3600

Charter One Pavilion, 33.
Northerly Island, 1300 S Linn White Dr
☎ 540-2668

Chicago Children's Museum, 14
700 E Grand Ave ☎ 527-1000

Chicago Cultural Center, 20.
78 E Washington St ☎ 346-3278

Chicago History Museum, 6.
1601 N Clark St ☎ 773/642-4600

Chicago Theater, 24.
175 N State St ☎ 462-6300

**Chicago Water Tower and
Pumping Station, 11.**
806 & 811 N Michigan Ave

Chinatown, 34.
Cermak St & Archer Ave

**DuSable Museum of
African American History, 37.**
740 E 56th Pl
☎ 773/947-0600

Field Museum of Natural History, 30.
1400 S Lake Shore Dr ☎ 922-9410

Grant Park, 28. Lakefront,
Roosevelt Rd to Randolph Rd

Greektown, 25.
Halstead St & Madison St

Harold Washington Library Center, 27.
400 S State St ☎ 747-4396

John G Shedd Aquarium, 31.
1200 S Lake Shore Dr ☎ 939-2426

John Hancock Observatory, 9.
875 N Michigan Ave ☎ 751-3681

Lincoln Park, 2.
Hollywood Ave to North Ave

Lincoln Park Zoo, 4.
2200 N Cannon Dr ☎ 742-2000

Magnificent Mile, 8.
Michigan Ave, Kinzie St to Oak St

Macy's, 19. 111 N State St ☎ 781-1000

Michigan Avenue Bridge, 16.
Michigan Ave & Wacker Dr

Millenium Park, 21.
Monroe St to Randolph St,
Michigan Ave to Columbus Dr
☎ 742-1168

Museum of Contemporary Art, 12.
220 E Chicago Ave ☎ 280-2660

**Museum of Science and
Industry, 35.** 5700 S Lake Shore
Dr ☎ 773/684-1414

**Peggy Notebaert
Nature Museum, 3.**
Fullerton Pkwy & Cannon Dr
☎ 773/755-5100

Navy Pier, 14.
600 E Grand Ave ☎ 595-PIER

Oak Street Beach, 7.
600N-1600N, Lakefront

River North Gallery District, 13.
Orleans to Wells Sts,
Erie St to Chicago Ave

Sears Tower, 26.
233 S Wacker Dr ☎ 875-9447

Skyline View, 29.
Museum Campus, 12th St and
Lake Shore Dr

State of Illinois Center, 17.
100 W Randolph St

Symphony Center, 23.
220 S Michigan Ave ☎ 294-3000

Tribune Tower, 15.
435 N Michigan Ave

United Center, 5. 1901 W Madison St
☎ 455-4500

University of Chicago, 36.
5801 S Ellis Ave ☎ 773/702-1234

Untitled, Picasso, 18.
W Washington St at N Dearborn

Water Tower Place, 10.
835 N Michigan Ave ☎ 440-3166.

Wrigley Field, 1. 1060 W Addison St
☎ 800/THE-CUBS

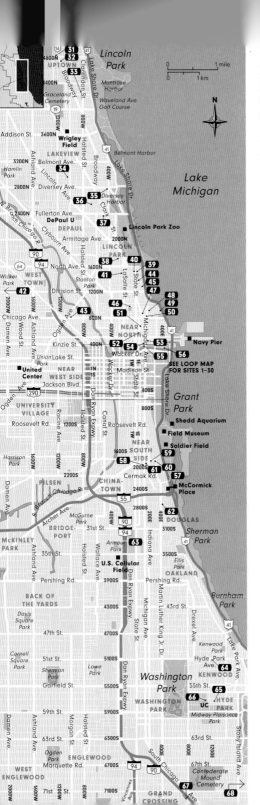

Listed by
Site Number

31 Uptown Theatre

32 Uptown Bank Bldg

33 Hutchinson Street Landmark District

34 H Rokham House

35 Elks National Veterans Memorial

36 St Clement's Church

37 Reebie Storage & Moving Co

38 Crilly Court

39 1500 N Astor St

40 Albert Madlener Residence

41 155 W Burton Place

42 Holy Trinity Cathedral

43 St John Cantius

44 Charnley-Persky House

45 Carl C Heisen House

46 Newberry Library

47 Archbishop Quigley Prep Seminary

48 John Hancock Building

49 860–880 N Lake Shore Dr

50 Chicago Water Tower/Pumping Stn

51 St James Episcopal Cathedral

52 Medinah Temple

53 Tribune Tower

54 Wrigley Building

55 Michigan Avenue Br

56 Centennial Fountain and Arc

57 McCormick Place

58 Second Presbyterian Church

59 J J Glessner House

60 W W Kimball Hse

61 Clarke House

62 Monument to the Great Migration

63 Illinois Institute of Technology Campus

64 I Heller House

65 Robie House

66 Univ of Chicago Quadrangles

67 Pullman

68 South Shore Cultural Center

Listed by Site Number

1 Marina City
2 75 E Wacker Dr
3 Carbon and
   Carbide Building
4 35 E Wacker Dr
5 333 W Wacker Dr
6 State of Illinois Ctr
7 Chicago Theater
8 Chicago Cultural Ctr
9 Reliance Building
10 *Miss Chicago*
11 *Untitled,* Picasso

12 Chicago Temple
13 Civic Opera Building
14 Old St. Patrick's
15 *Dawn Shadows*
16 Sears Tower
17 135 S LaSalle St
18 The Rookery
19 Chicago Board of
   Trade
20 Chicago
   Metropolitan
   Correction Center

21 Harold Washington
   Library Center
22 Monadnock Building
23 *Flamingo*
24 Marquette Building
25 *The Four Seasons*
26 Inland Steel Building
27 Carson Pirie Scott & Co
28 Santa Fe Center
29 Auditorium Building
30 Buckingham
   Fountain

Listed Alphabetically

**Albert Madlener Residence, (Graham
Foundation for Advanced Studies in
the Fine Arts),** 40.
4 W Burton Pl ☎ 573-1365

**Archbishop Quigley
Preparatory Seminary,** 47.
Pearson and Rush Sts

Auditorium Building, 29.
430 S Michigan Ave

Buckingham Fountain, 30.
Congress Pkwy at Columbus Dr

Carbon and Carbide Building, 3.
230 N Michigan Ave

Carl C Heisen House, 45.
1250 N Lake Shore Dr

Carson Pirie Scott & Co, 27.
1 S State St

Centennial Fountain and Arc, 56.
300 E McClurg Court

Charnley-Persky House, 44.
1365 N Astor St ☎ 915-0105

Chicago Board of Trade Building, 19.
141 W Jackson Blvd ☎ 435-3590

Chicago Cultural Center, 8.
78 E Washington St ☎ 346-3278

**Chicago Metropolitan
Correctional Center,** 20.
71 W Van Buren St

**Chicago Temple (First United
Methodist Church of Chicago),** 12.
77 W Washington St ☎ 236-4548

Chicago Theater, 7.
175 N State St ☎ 462-6318

**Chicago Water Tower and
Pumping Station,** 50.
806 & 811 N Michigan Ave

Civic Opera Building, 13.
20 N Wacker Dr ☎ 332-2244

Listed Alphabetically

Clarke House, 61.
1827 S Indiana Ave ☎ 326–1480

Crilly Court, 38. North Park Ave & Wells St, St Paul Ave & Eugenie

Dawn Shadows, Nevelson, 15.
200 W Madison St

860-880 N Lake Shore Dr, 49.

Elks National Veterans Memorial, 35.
2750 N Lakeview Ave ☎ 773/755-4876

1500 N Astor St (Patterson-McCormick Mansion), 39.
20 E Burton Place

Flamingo, Calder, 23.
Dearborn St between Adams & Jackson Sts

The Four Seasons, Chagall, 25.
Dearborn and Monroe Sts

Frederick C Robie House, 65.
5757 S Woodlawn Ave ☎ 773/834-1847

Harold Washington Library Center, 21.
400 S State St ☎ 747-4396

Henry Rohkam House, 34.
1048 W Oakdale Ave

Holy Trinity Cathedral, 42.
1121 N Leavitt St ☎ 773/486-6064

Hutchinson Street Landmark District, 33. Hutchinson St between Marine Dr & Hazel St

Illinois Institute of Technology Campus, 63.
3201 S State St ☎ 567-5014

Inland Steel Building, 26.
30 W Monroe St

Isidore Heller House, 63.
5132 S Woodlawn Ave

John Hancock Building, 48.
875 N Michigan Ave ☎ 751-3681

John J Glessner House, 59.
1800 S Prairie Ave ☎ 326-1480

Marina City, 1. 300 N State St

Marquette Building, 24.
140 S Dearborn St

McCormick Place, 57.
2301 S Lake Shore Dr ☎ 791-6300

Medinah Temple, 52.
600 N Wabash Ave

Michigan Avenue Bridge, 55.
Michigan Ave & Wacker Dr

Miss Chicago, Miro, 10.
Washington and Dearborn Sts

Monadnock Building, 22.
53 W Jackson Blvd

Monument to the Great Migration, 62.
26th Pl and Martin Luther King Dr

Newberry Library, 46.
60 W Walton St ☎ 943-9090

Old St Patrick's Roman Catholic Church, 14.
700 W Adams St ☎ 648-1021

135 S LaSalle St, 17.
LaSalle & Adams Sts

155 W Burton Place, 41. Burton Place between LaSalle & Wells Sts

Pullman, 67. 111th and 115th Sts, Cottage Grove and Langley Aves
☎ 773/785-8901

Reebie Storage & Moving Co., 37.
2325 N Clark St

Reliance Building, 9. 32 N State St

The Rookery, 18. 209 S LaSalle St

St Clement's Church, 36.
646 W Deming Place ☎ 773/281-0371

St James Episcopal Cathedral, 51.
65 E Huron ☎ 787-7360.

St John Cantius Roman Catholic Church, 43. 825 N Carpenter St
☎ 243-7373

Santa Fe Center, 28.
80 E Jackson Blvd

Sears Tower, 16.
233 S Wacker Dr ☎ 875-9447

Second Presbyterian Church, 58.
1936 S Michigan Ave ☎ 225-4951

75 E Wacker Dr, 2.

South Shore Cultural Center, 66.
7059 S Shore Dr ☎ 773/256-0149

State of Illinois Center, 6.
100 W Randolph St

35 E Wacker Dr, 4.

333 W Wacker Dr, 5.

Tribune Tower, 53.
435 N Michigan Ave ☎ 222-3994

University of Chicago Quadrangles, 66. Ellis and University Aves, E 57th and E 59th Sts

Untitled, Picasso, 11.
Washington and Dearborn Sts

Uptown Bank Building, 32.
4707 N Broadway

Uptown Theatre, 31. 4814 N Broadway

William W Kimball House, 60.
1801 S Prairie Ave

Wrigley Building, 54.
400-410 N Michigan Ave

Listed by Site Number

1 O B Balch Home
2 W G Fricke Home
3 Edwin C Cheney Home
4 Rollin Furbeck Home
5 Frank Lloyd Wright Home and Studio
6 R P Parker Home
7 T H Gale Home
8 Walter H Gale Home
9 Moore-Dugal Home
10 A B Heurtley Home
11 Mrs. T. H. Gale Home
12 Ernest Hemingway Birthplace
13 Hills-DeCaro Home
14 G W Furbeck Home
15 Hemingway Museum
16 F W Thomas Home
17 Oak Park Visitors Center
18 Unity Temple
19 Historical Society of Oak Park & River Forest
19 Pleasant Home
20 Oak Park Conservatory
21 Brookfield Zoo

Listed Alphabetically

Arthur B Heurtley Home, 10.
318 N Forest Ave

Brookfield Zoo, 21. 8400 31st St, Brookfield ☎ 708/485-0263

Edwin H Cheney Home, 3.
520 N East Ave

Ernest Hemingway Birthplace, 12.
339 N Oak Park Ave ☎ 708/848-2222

Ernest Hemingway Museum, 15.
200 N Oak Park Ave ☎ 708/848-2222

Frank Lloyd Wright Home and Studio, 5.
951 Chicago Ave ☎ 708/848-1976

Frank W Thomas Home, 16.
210 N Forest Ave

George W Furbeck Home, 14.
223 N Euclid Ave

Hills-DeCaro, 13. 313 Forest Ave

Historical Society of Oak Park & River Forest, 19.
217 S Home Ave ☎ 708/848-6755

Moore-Dugal Home, 9.
333 N Forest Ave

Mrs Thomas H Gale Home, 11.
6 Elizabeth Court

Oak Park Conservatory, 20.
615 W Garfield St ☎ 708/725-2450

Oak Park Visitors Center, 17.
158 N Forest Ave ☎ 708/848-1500
☎ 1-888-OAK-PARK

Oscar B Balch Home, 1.
611 N Kenilworth Ave

Pleasant Home (John Farson Home), 19.
217 S Home Ave ☎ 708/383-2654

Robert P Parker Home, 6.
1019 W Chicago Ave

Rollin Furbeck Home, 4.
515 N Fair Oaks Ave

Thomas H Gale Home, 7.
1027 W Chicago Ave

Unity Temple, 18.
875 Lake St ☎ 708/383-8873

Walter H Gale Home, 8.
1031 W Chicago Ave

William G Fricke Home, 2.
540 N Fair Oaks Ave

Listed by Site Number

1 George L Miller House
2 KAM Isaiah Israel Congregation
3 Isidore Heller House
4 Hyde Park Art Center
5 David and Alfred Smart Museum of Art
6 Court Theatre
7 *Nuclear Energy*
8 DuSable Museum of African American History
9 John Crerar Library
10 Renaissance Society
11 Bond Chapel
12 Joseph Regenstein Library
13 Reynolds Club/Mandel Hall
14 University Church
15 Hyde Park Historical Society
16 Doc Films/Max Palevsky Cinema
17 Museum of Science and Industry
18 Powell's Bookstore
19 O'Gara & Wilson Booksellers
20 57th Street Books
21 Frederick C Robie House
22 Seminary Co-Op Bookstore
22 Chicago Theological Seminary
23 Oriental Institute
24 Rockefeller Memorial Chapel
25 *Fountain of Time*
26 School of Social Service Administration
27 Jackson Park

Listed Alphabetically

Bond Chapel, 11. 1025 E 58th St

Chicago Theological Seminary, 22. 5757 S University Ave ☎ 773/752–5757

Court Theatre, 6. 5535 S Ellis Ave ☎ 773/753–4472

David and Alfred Smart Museum of Art, 5. 5500 S Greenwood Ave ☎ 773/702–0200

Doc Films/Max Palevsky Cinema, 16. Ida Noyes Hall, 1212 E 59th St ☎ 773/702–8575

DuSable Museum of African American History, 8. 740 E 56th Pl ☎ 773/947–0600

57th Street Books, 20. 1301 E 57th St ☎ 773/684–1300

Fountain of Time, Taft, 25. Midway Plaisance, West of Cottage Grove Ave

Frederick C Robie House, 21. 5757 S Woodlawn Ave ☎ 708/848–1976

George L Miller House, 1. 4800 S Kimbark Ave

Court Theatre, 6. 5535 S Ellis Ave ☎ 773/753–4472

Hyde Park Art Center, 4. 5020 S Cornell Ave ☎ 773/324–5520

Isidore Heller House, 3. 5132 S Woodlawn Ave

Jackson Park, 27. E 56th–67th Sts, S Stony Island to Lake Michigan ☎ 747–6187

John Crerar Library, 9. 5730 S Ellis Ave ☎ 773/702–7715

Joseph Regenstein Library, 12. 1100 E 57th St

KAM Isaiah Israel Congregation, 2. 1100 E Hyde Park Blvd ☎ 773/924–1234

Museum of Science and Industry, 17. 5700 S Lake Shore Dr ☎ 773/684–1414

Nuclear Energy, Moore, 7. Ellis Ave between 56th & 57th Sts

O'Gara & Wilson Booksellers, 19. 1448 E 57th St ☎ 773/363–0993

Oriental Institute, 23. 1155 E 58th St ☎ 773/702–9514

Powell's Bookstore, 18. 1501 E 57th St ☎ 773/955–7780

Renaissance Society, 10. 5811 S Ellis Ave ☎ 773/702–8670

Reynolds Club/Mandel Hall, 13. 1131 E 57th St ☎ 773/702–7300

Rockefeller Memorial Chapel, 24. 5850 S Woodlawn Ave ☎ 773/702–7059.

School of Social Service Administration, 26. 969 E 60th St

Seminary Co-Op Bookstore, 22. 5757 S University Ave ☎ 773/752–4381

University Church, 14. 5655 S University Ave ☎ 773/363–8142

Listed by Site Number

1 Chicago Botanic Garden

2 Kohl Children's Museum

3 Baha'i House of Worship

4 Kendall-Mitchell Museum of the American Indian

5 Ladd Memorial Arboretum and Ecology Center

6 Grosse Pointe Lighthouse and Maritime Museum

7 Shakespeare Garden

8 Mary and Leigh Block Gallery

9 Northwestern University

10 Frances E Willard House/National Women's Christian Temperance Union Headquarters

11 Merrick Rose Garden

12 Evanston Historical Society/Charles G Dawes Home

13 Noyes Cultural Arts Center

14 Evanston Arts Depot

Listed Alphabetically

Baha'i House of Worship, 3.
100 Linden Ave, Wilmette
☎ 847/853-2300

Chicago Botanic Garden, 1.
Lake Cook Road and Rte. 41, Glencoe
☎ 847/835-5440

Evanston Arts Depot, 14.
600 Main St ☎ 847/328-2204

Evanston Historical Society/ Charles G Dawes Home, 12.
225 Greenwood Ave ☎ 847/475-3410

Frances E Willard House/National Women's Christian Temperance Union Headquarters, 10.
1730 Chicago Ave ☎ 847/328-7500

Grosse Pointe Lighthouse and Maritime Museum, 6.
2601 N. Sheridan Rd ☎ 847/328-6961

Kendall-Mitchell Museum of the American Indian, 4.
3001 Central St ☎ 847/475-1030

Kohl Children's Museum, 2.
2100 Patriot Blvd, Glenview
☎ 847/832-6600

Ladd Memorial Arboretum and Ecology Center, 5.
2024 McCormick Rd ☎ 847/864-5181

Mary and Leigh Block Museum of Art, 8. 40 Arts Circle Drive ☎ 847/491-4000

Merrick Rose Garden, 11.
Oak Ave & Lake St ☎ 847/866-2900

Northwestern University, 9.
633 Clark St ☎ 847/491-3741

Noyes Cultural Arts Center, 13.
927 Noyes St ☎ 847/448-8260

Shakespeare Garden, 7.
2121 Sheridan Rd

Listed by Site Number

1 Northshore Center for the Performing Arts

1 Old Orchard Shopping Center

2 Holocaust Memorial Museum

3 Skokie Northshore Sculpture Park

4 Emily Oaks Nature Center

5 The Exploritorium

6 Skokie Heritage Museum and Log Cabin/Skokie Historical Society

7 Skokie Theater

Listed Alphabetically

Emily Oaks Nature Center, 4.
4650 Brummel St ☎ 847/677-7001

The Exploritorium, 5.
4701 Oakton St
☎ 847/674-1500, ext 2744

Holocaust Memorial Foundation Museum, 2.
4255 Main St ☎ 847/677-4640

Northshore Center for the Performing Arts, 1.
9501 Skokie Blvd ☎ 847/673-6300

Old Orchard Shopping Center, 1.
Old Orchard Rd & Skokie Blvd
☎ 847/674-7070

Skokie Heritage Museum and Log Cabin, 6.
8031 Floral Ave ☎ 847/677-6672 / 847/674-1500, ext 3020

Skokie Historical Society, 6.
8031 Floral Ave ☎ 847/673-1888 / 847/674-1500 ext 3020

Skokie Northshore Sculpture Park, 3.
McCormick Blvd between Dempster St and Touhy Ave ☎ 847/679-4265

Skokie Theater, 7.
7924 N Lincoln Ave ☎ 847/677-7761

Listed by Site Number

1 Willie Dixon's Blues Heaven

2 Quinn Chapel AME Church

3 Bronzeville Visitor Information Center Gallery

4 Monument to the Great Migration

5 Olivet Baptist Church

6 South Side Community Art Center

7 Victory

8 Eighth Regiment Armory

9 Chicago Bee

10 Swift Mansion

11 Oscar Stanton De Priest Home

12 Elijah Muhammad Home

13 Rainbow PUSH

14 DuSable Museum Of African American History

15 Oak Woods Cemetary

16 Mosque Maryam

Listed Alphabetically

Bronzeville Visitor Information Center Gallery, 3.
411 E 35 St ☎ 773/373-2842

Chicago Bee Building, 9.
3647-55 S State St

DuSable Museum of African American History, 14.
740 E 56th Pl ☎ 773/947-0600

Eighth Regiment Armory, 8.
3533 S Giles St

Elijah Muhammad Home, 12.
4847 S Woodlawn Ave

Monument to the Great Migration, 4.
26th Pl and Martin Luther King Dr

Mosque Maryam, 16. 7351 S Stony Island Ave ☎ 773/324-6000

Oak Woods Cemetery, 15.
67th St and Cottage Grove Ave
☎ 773/288-3800

Olivet Baptist Church, 5.
3101 Martin L King Dr ☎ 528-0124

Oscar Stanton De Priest Home, 11.
4536-38 S Martin L King Dr

Quinn Chapel AME Church, 2.
2401 S. Wabash Ave ☎ 791-1846

Rainbow PUSH, 13.
930 E 50th St ☎ 773/373-3366

South Side Community Art Center, 6. 3831 S Michigan Ave
☎ 773/373-1026

Swift Mansion, 10.
4500 S Michigan Ave

Victory, Monument for the 93rd Division, 7.
Martin L King Dr at 35th St

Willie Dixon's Blues Heaven, 1.
2120 S Michigan Ave ☎ 808-1286

Mosques

Listed by Site Number

1 Ner Tamid Congregation of North Town

2 Islamic Center of Chicago

3 Rosehill Cemetery

4 Emanuel Congregation

5 St Ita's Church

6 Edgewater Presbyterian Church

7 All Saints Episcopal Church

8 St Mary of the Lake

9 Graceland Cemetery

10 Temple Sholom

11 Anshe Emet Synagogue

12 Our Lady of Mount Carmel Church

13 Wellington Ave United Church of Christ

14 St Alphonsus Redemptorist

15 St Clement's Church

16 St. George Greek Orthodox Church

17 St Paul's United Church of Christ

18 Church of Our Savior

19 St Vincent de Paul Church

20 St Mary of the Angels

21 First Bethlehem Lutheran Church

22 Midwest Buddhist Temple

23 St Michael's Church

24 Moody Church

25 St Chrysostom's Episcopal Church

26 Holy Trinity Cathedral

27 St Nicholas Ukranian Catholic Cathedral

28 Lake Shore Drive Synagogue

29 Chicago Sinai Congregation

30 Fourth Presbyterian Church

31 Holy Name Cathedral

32 St James Cathedral

33 Seventeenth Church of Christ Scientist

34 First United Methodist Church (Chicago Temple)

35 St Peter's Church

36 Chicago Loop Synagogue

37 Old St. Patrick's Church

38 First Baptist Congregational

39 Greek Orthodox Church of St Basil

40 St Pius

41 Old St. Mary's Church

42 Second Presbyterian Church

43 Quinn Chapel AME

44 Olivet Baptist Church

45 Grant Memorial AME Church

46 KAM Isaiah Israel Congregation

47 First Unitarian Church of Chicago

48 Rockefeller Memorial Chapel

49 Oak Woods Cemetery

50 Mosque Maryam

Listed Alphabetically

Anshe Emet Synagogue, 11.
3751 N Broadway ☎ 773/281-1423
Conservative Jewish

All Saints Episcopal Church, 7.
4550 N Hermitage Ave
☎ 773/561-0111

Chicago Loop Synagogue, 36.
16 S Clark St ☎ 346-7370.
Traditional Jewish

Chicago Sinai Congregation, 29.
15 W Delaware Pl ☎ 867-7000.
Reform Jewish

Church of Our Savior, 18.
530 W Fullerton Pkwy
☎ 773/549-3832 Episcopal

Edgewater Presbyterian Church, 6.
1020 W Bryn Mawr Ave
☎ 773/561-4748

Emanuel Congregation, 4.
5959 N Sheridan Rd
☎ 773/561-5173 Reform Jewish

First Baptist Congregational Church, 38.
1613 W Washington Blvd ☎ 243-8047

First Bethlehem Lutheran Church, 21. 1649 W LeMoyne St
☎ 773/276-2338

First Unitarian Church of Chicago, 47. 5650 S Woodlawn Ave
☎ 773/324-4100

First United Methodist Church of Chicago (Chicago Temple), 34.
77 W Washington St ☎ 236-4548

Fourth Presbyterian Church, 30.
126 E Chestnut St ☎ 787-4570

Listed Alphabetically

Grant Memorial AME Church, 45.
4017 S Drexel Blvd ☎ 773/285–5819

**Greek Orthodox
Church of St Basil, 39.**
733 S Ashland Ave ☎ 243–3738

Holy Name Cathedral, 31.
735 N State St ☎ 787–8040.
Roman Catholic

Holy Trinity Cathedral, 26.
1121 N. Leavitt St ☎ 773/486–6064.
Russian Orthodox

Islamic Center of Chicago, 2.
5933 N Lincoln Ave ☎ 773/989–9330

KAM Isaiah Israel Congregation, 46.
1100 E Hyde Park Blvd
☎ 773/924–1234. Reform Jewish

Lake Shore Drive Synagogue, 28.
70 E Elm St ☎ 337–6811.
Traditional Jewish

Midwest Buddhist Temple, 22.
435 Menomonee St ☎ 943–7801

Moody Church, 24. 1609 N LaSalle Dr
☎ 943–0466. Non-denominational

Mosque Maryam, 50.
7351 S Stony Island Ave
☎ 773/324–6000. Nation of Islam

**Ner Tamid Congregation of
North Town, 1.**
2754 W Rosemont Ave
☎ 773/465–6090.
Conservative Jewish

Old St. Mary's Church, 41.
1500 S Michigan Ave ☎ 922–3444
Roman Catholic

Old St. Patrick's Church, 37.
700 W Adams St ☎ 648–1021.
Roman Catholic

Olivet Baptist Church, 44.
3101 S Martin Luther King Dr
☎ 528–0124

**Our Lady of Mount
Carmel Church, 12.**
690 W Belmont Ave
☎ 773/525–0453. Roman Catholic

Quinn Chapel AME, 43.
2401 S Wabash Ave ☎ 791–1846

Rockefeller Memorial Chapel, 48.
5850 S Woodlawn Ave
☎ 773/702–2100. Ecumenical

**St Alphonsus
Redemptorist Church, 14.**
1429 W Wellington Ave
☎ 773/525–0709. Roman Catholic

**St Chrysostom's Episcopal Church,
25.** 1424 N Dearborn Pkwy
☎ 944–1083

St Clement's Church, 15.
642 W. Deming Pl
☎ 773/281–0371. Roman
Catholic

**St George Greek
Orthodox Church, 16.**
2701 N Sheffield Ave ☎ 773/525–1793

St Ita's Church, 5. 1220 W Catalpa Ave
☎ 773/561–5343. Roman Catholic

St James Cathedral, 32.
65 E Huron St ☎ 787–7360. Episcopal

St Mary of the Angels Church, 20.
1850 N Hermitage Ave
☎ 773/278–2644. Roman Catholic

St Mary of the Lake, 8.
4200 N Sheridan Rd ☎ 773/472–3711.
Roman Catholic

St Michael's Church, 23.
447 W Eugenie St ☎ 642–2498.
Roman Catholic

**St Nicholas Ukranian
Catholic Cathedral, 27.**
2238 W Rice St ☎ 773/276–4537

St Paul's United Church of Christ, 17.
2335 N Orchard St ☎ 773/348–3829

St Peter's Church, 35.
110 W Madison St ☎ 372–5111.
Roman Catholic

St Pius, 40. 1919 S Ashland Ave
☎ 226–6161. Roman Catholic

St Vincent de Paul Church, 19.
1010 W Webster Ave ☎ 773/325–8610.
Roman Catholic

Second Presbyterian Church, 42.
1936 S Michigan Ave ☎ 225–4951

**Seventeenth Church of Christ
Scientist, 33.**
55 E Wacker Dr ☎ 236–4671

Temple Sholom, 10.
3480 N Lake Shore Dr
☎ 773/525–4707. Reform Jewish

**Wellington Ave United
Church of Christ, 13.**
615 W Wellington Ave
☎ 773/935–0642

CEMETERIES

Graceland Cemetery, 9.
4001 N Clark St ☎ 773/525–1105

Oak Woods Cemetery, 49.
1035 E 67th St ☎ 773/288–3800

Rosehill Cemetery, 3. 800 N
Ravenswood Ave
☎ 773/561–5940

MAP **34** Museums/Downtown, Near North &

Diversey Harbor

1

Lincoln Park Zoo

N. Branch Chicago R.

Fullerton Ave.

Lincoln Ave.

Clark St.

2400N

DePaul U

DEPAUL

Clybourn Ave.

Armitage Ave.

2000N

LINCOLN
PARK

2

3

North Ave. 1600N

LaSalle St.

State St.

US 41

Milwaukee Ave.

I-90
I-94

North Ave.

64

Wicker
Park

Halsted St.

Stanton
Park

Division St. 1200N

UKRAINIAN
VILLAGE

Division St.

1200W

2000W

1600W

NEAR
NORTH

6

7

Western Ave.

800N Chicago Ave.

Leavitt St.

Damen Ave.

Wood St.

Ashland Ave.

Ogden Ave.

800W

Water
Tower

11

NEAR
NORTH

Michigan Ave.

400E

8

Navy P

5

400N Kinzie St.

Union
Park

Lake St.

400N

9

Wacker Dr.

1W

1E

10

001N
001S

United
Center

19 NEAR
WEST SIDE

1N
1S

Wacker Dr.

Madison St.

LOOP

Adams St.

State St.

12

Lake Shore Dr.

Grant
Park

Eisenhower Expwy.

290

Jackson Blvd.

Dan Ryan Expwy.

University of
Illinois/Chicago

400S

13

14

UNIVERSITY
VILLAGE

Racine Ave.

18

Halsted St.

800S

15

Shedd Aquariu

Ogden Ave.

Roosevelt Rd.

1200S

Roosevelt Rd.

1W

1E

17

Field Museum

2400W

Harrison
Park

20

1600W

1200W

800W

Canal St.

Soldier Field

NEAR
SOUTH
SIDE

21

Western Ave.

Damen Ave.

PILSEN

1600S

CHINA-
TOWN

2000S

Cermak Rd.

200S

McCormick
Place

2200S

S. Branch Chicago R.

2400S

55

2800S

200E

400E

US 41

DOUGLAS

3100S

Sherman
Park

55

Archer Ave.

McGurne
Park

BRIDGE-
PORT

31st St.

400W

I-90
I-94

Armour
Park

Illinois
Institute of
Technology

Indiana Ave.

Ellis
Park

McKINLEY
PARK

Ashland Ave.

35th St.

Halsted St.

Wallace Ave.

U.S. Cellular
Field

Dan Ryan Expwy.

3500S

OAKLAND

Western Ave.

3900S

Pershing Rd.

Michigan Ave.

Martin Luther King Jr. Dr.

43rd St.

Drexel Ave.

4300S

State St.

4700S

To
HYDE PARK

Washington
Park

S Ellis Ave.

22

S Woodlawn Ave.

S Dorchester Ave.

E 55th St.

23

S Martin Luther King Jr. Dr.

S Cottage Grove Ave.

24

University of Chicago
Midway Plaisance
Park

25

E 60th St.

Jackson
Park

Hyde Park Area

1 mil

1 km

N

Listed by Site Number

1. Peggy Notebaert Nature Museum
2. Chicago History Museum
3. International Museum of Surgical Science
4. Polish Museum of America
5. Ukranian Institute of Modern Art
6. Loyola University Chicago Museum of Art
7. Museum of Contemporary Art
8. Chicago Children's Museum
9. McCormick Freedom Museum
10. Chicago Cultural Center
11. Richard H. Driehaus Museum
12. Art Institute of Chicago
13. Museum of Contemporary Photography
14. Spertus Museum
15. John G Shedd Aquarium
16. Adler Planetarium and Astronomy Museum
17. Field Museum of Natural History
18. Hull House Museum
19. Museum of Holography
20. National Museum of Mexican Art
21. Clarke House Museum
21. Glessner House Museum
21. National Vietnam Veterans Museum of Art
22. David and Alfred Smart Museum of Art
23. DuSable Museum of African American History
24. Oriental Institute
25. Museum of Science and Industry

Listed Alphabetically

Adler Planetarium and Astronomy Museum, 16.
1300 S Lake Shore Dr ☎ 922-STAR

Art Institute of Chicago, 12.
111 S Michigan Ave ☎ 443-3600

Chicago Children's Museum, 8.
Navy Pier, 700 E Grand Ave ☎ 527-1000

Chicago Cultural Center, 10.
78 E Washington St ☎ 346-3278

Chicago History Museum, 2.
1601 N Clark St ☎ 642-4600

Clarke House Museum, 21.
1827 S Indiana Ave ☎ 326-1480

David and Alfred Smart Museum of Art, 22.
5500 S Greenwood Ave ☎ 773/702-0200

DuSable Museum of African American History, 23.
740 E 56th Pl ☎ 773/947-0600

Field Museum of Natural History, 17.
1400 S Lake Shore Dr ☎ 922-9410

Hull House Museum, 18.
800 S Halsted St ☎ 413-5353

International Museum of Surgical Science, 3.
1524 N Lake Shore Dr ☎ 642-6502

Glessner House Museum, 21.
1800 S Prairie Ave ☎ 326-1480

John G Shedd Aquarium, 15.
1200 S Lake Shore Dr ☎ 939-2426

Loyola University Chicago Museum of Art, 6.
820 N Michigan Ave ☎ 915-7600

McCormick Freedom Museum, 9.
435 N Michigan Ave ☎ 222-4860

Museum of Contemporary Art, 7.
220 E Chicago Ave ☎ 280-2660

Museum of Contemporary Photography, 13.
Columbia College, 600 S Michigan Ave ☎ 344-7779

Museum of Holography, 19.
1134 W Washington St ☎ 226-1007

Museum of Science and Industry, 25.
5700 S Lake Shore Dr ☎ 773/684-1414

National Museum of Mexican Art, 20.
1852 W 19th St ☎ 738-1503

National Vietnam Veterans Museum of Art, 21.
1801 S Indiana Ave ☎ 326-0270

Oriental Institute, 24.
1155 E 58th St ☎ 773/702-9514

Peggy Notebaert Nature Museum, 1.
Fullerton Pkwy & Cannon Dr ☎ 773/755-5100

Polish Museum of America, 4.
984 N Milwaukee Ave ☎ 773/384-3352

Richard H. Direhaus Museum, 11.
40 E Erie St ☎ 932-8665

Spertus Museum, 14.
610 S Michigan Ave ☎ 322-1700

Ukranian Institute of Modern Art, 5.
2320 W Chicago Ave ☎ 773/227-5522

Listed by Site Number

27 Martin D'Arcy Gallery of Art

28 Swedish-American Museum Center

29 Bronzeville Children's Museum

30 Balzekas Museum of Lithuanian Culture

31 A Philip Randolph Pullman Porter National Museum

Listed Alphabetically

A Philip Randolph Pullman Porter Museum, 31.
10406 S Maryland Ave
☎ 773/928-3935

Balzekas Museum of Lithuanian Culture, 30.
6500 S Pulaski Rd ☎ 773/582-6500

Bronzeville Children's Musuem, 29.
9301 S Stony Island Ave ☎ 773/721-9301

Martin D'Arcy Gallery of Art, 27.
Loyola University, 6525 N Sheridan Ave
☎ 773/508-2679

Swedish-American Museum Center, 28. 5211 N Clark St ☎ 773/728-8111

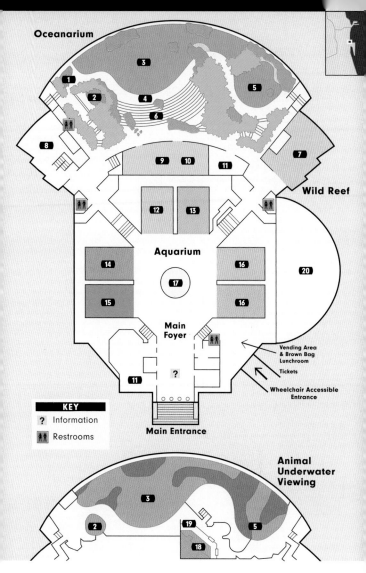

Oceanarium

- 1
- 2
- 3
- 4
- 5
- 6
- 7
- 8

Wild Reef

- 9
- 10
- 11
- 12
- 13

Aquarium

- 14
- 15
- 16
- 16
- 17
- 20

Main Foyer

Vending Area
& Brown Bag
Lunchroom

Tickets

Wheelchair Accessible
Entrance

- 11
- ?

KEY

? Information

🚻 Restrooms

Main Entrance

Animal Underwater Viewing

- 2
- 3
- 5
- 18
- 19

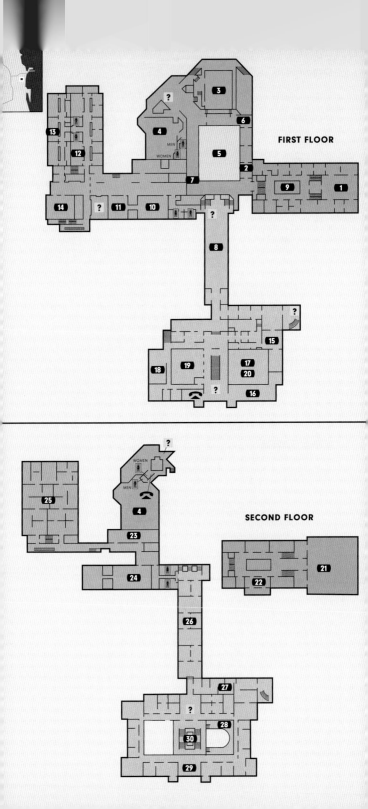

FIRST FLOOR

SECOND FLOOR

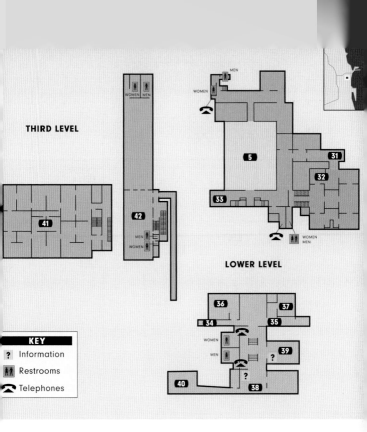

THIRD LEVEL

LOWER LEVEL

KEY
? Information
Restrooms
Telephones

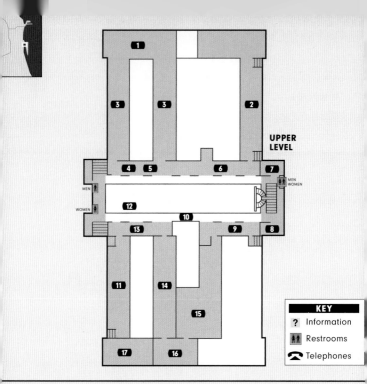

UPPER LEVEL

KEY
? Information
👫 Restrooms
☎ Telephones

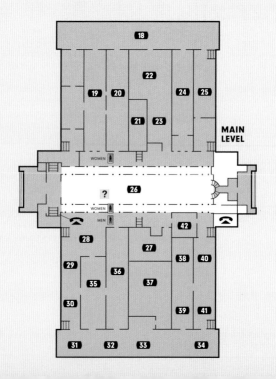

MAIN LEVEL

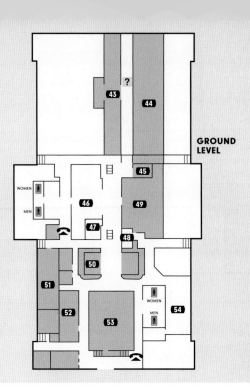

GROUND LEVEL

Listed by Site Number

1 Elizabeth Morse Genius Dinosaur Hall
2 Plants of the World
3 Evolving Planet
4 McDonald's Fossil Prep Lab
5 The Sue Store
6 Moving Earth
7 Hall of Jades
8 Hall of Gems
9 China
10 Japanese Lacquer
11 Special Exhibits
12 More on Sue
13 Tibet
14 Pacific Spirits
15 Traveling the Pacific
16 Maori Meeting House
17 Marae Gallery
18 Northwest Coast & Arctic Peoples
19 The Ancient Americas

20 Yates Exhibition Center
21 Holleb Exhibition Gallery
22 Pawnee Earth Lodge
23 Webber Gallery
24 North American Indians
25 Museum Store
26 Stanley Field Hall
27 Africa Resource Center
28 Nature Walk
29 North American Birds
30 World of Birds
31 World of Mammals
32 Tsavo Lions
33 Rice Gallery
34 Mammals of Africa
35 Messages from the Wilderness
36 Mammals of Asia
37 Africa

38 Reptiles & Amphibians
39 Bird Habitats
40 What is an Animal?
41 Animal Biology
42 Inside Ancient Egypt
43 Crown Family Play Lab
44 Underground Adventure
45 Insects
46 The Siragusa Center
47 Man-eater of Mfuwe
48 Bushman
49 Inside Ancient Egypt
50 First Aid Center
51 Education Department
52 Harris & Webber Resource Centers
53 James Simpson Theatre
54 McDonald's

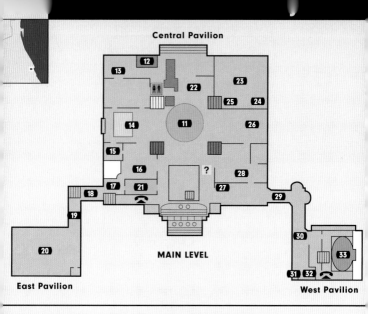

Central Pavilion

MAIN LEVEL

East Pavilion

West Pavilion

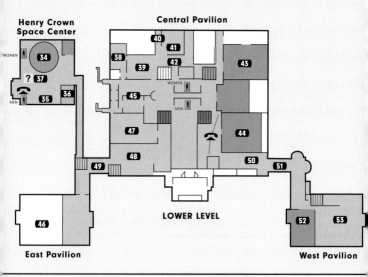

Henry Crown Space Center

Central Pavilion

WOMEN

MEN

LOWER LEVEL

East Pavilion

West Pavilion

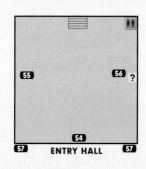

ENTRY HALL

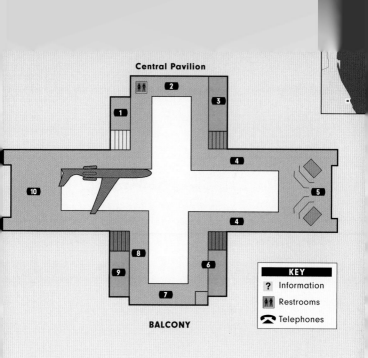

Central Pavilion

1

2

3

10

4

5

4

8

6

9

7

KEY

? Information

Restrooms

Telephones

BALCONY

Listed by Site Number

1 Reusable City
2 Education Labs
3 Regenstein Hall of Chemistry
4 Grainger Hall of Basic Science
5 Prenatal Development
6 You! The Experience
7 You! The Experience
8 You! The Experience
10 Take Flight
11 Rotunda
12 Finnigan's Ice Cream Parlor
13 Yesterday's Main Street
14 The Great Train
15 Baby Chicks
16 Genetics: Decoding Life
17 Out of the Vault
18 Spaceport
19 Navy
20 Flight Simulators
21 Members' Lounge
22 Coal Mine
23 Petroleum Planet
24 Toymaker 3000
25 Enterprise

26 Special Exhibits
27 Networld
28 Science Rediscovered
29 Whispering Gallery
30 Imaging
31 Mystery Lab
32 Virtual Reality
33 3-D Theater
34 Omnimax Theater
35 Smart Home: Green & Wired
36 Shop
37 Henry Crown Space Center
38 Plumbing
39 Energy Lab
40 Yesterday's Firefighters
41 Colleen Moore's Fairy Castle
42 Science Theater
43 Brain Food Court
44 Café Brain Food
45 Farm Tech
46 U-505 Submarine
47 Idea Factory
48 Circus
49 Eye Spy

50 Exploring the Collection
51 Ships
52 Reserved Group Dining
53 Group Center
54 Pioneer Zephyr
55 Shop
56 Tickets
57 Parking Garage

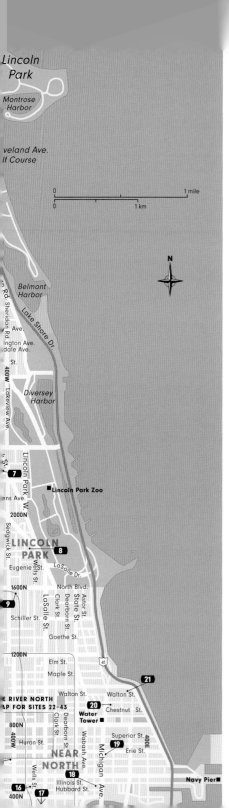

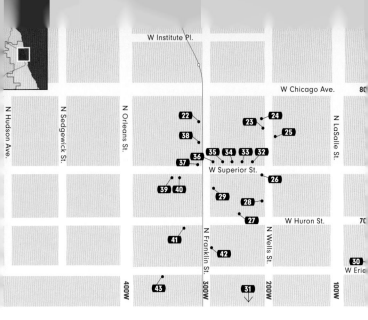

River North Detail Listed by Site Number

22 Eastern Gallery
22 Byron Roche
23 Carl Hammer Gallery
24 Portals, Ltd
25 Roy Boyd Gallery
26 Jean Albano Gallery
26 Josef Glimer Gallery Ltd.
26 Maya Polsky Gallery
27 Andrew Hollingsworth
28 Addington Gallery
28 Mongerson Galleries
29 Robert Henry Adams Fine Art
30 Andora Gallery
31 Gallery 500 Wells

32 Perimeter Gallery
33 Ann Nathan Gallery
34 Zygman Voss
35 Aboriginal Art Collection
35 Gruen Galleries
35 Habatat Galleries
36 I space
36 Marx-Saunders Gallery, Ltd
36 Schneider Gallery
36 Vale Craft Gallery
37 Catherine Edelman Gallery
37 Judy A Saslow Gallery
37 Andrew Bae Gallery
37 David Weinberg Gallery
37 Zg Gallery

38 Mary Bell Gallery
38 Melanee Cooper
39 Printworks Gallery
39 Stephen Daiter Gallery
40 Lydon Fine Art, Inc
41 Kass/Meridian
41 Zolla/Lieberman Gallery
42 Aldo Castillo Gallery
43 Gallery Stuart Rodgers

Art Galleries Listed Alphabetically

Aboriginal Art Collection, 35.
226 W Superior ☎ 475-9766

Addington Gallery, 28.
704 N Wells St ☎ 664-3406

Aldo Castillo Gallery, 42.
675 N Franklin ☎ 337-2536

Alfredena Gallery, 15.
434 W Ontario ☎ 944-4340

Andora Gallery, 30.
77 W Huron ☎ 274-3747

Byron Roche, 22.
750 N Franklin St ☎ 654-0144

Andrew Bae, 37.
300 W Superior St ☎ 335-8601

Andrew Hollingsworth, 27.
222 W Huron ☎ 440-9554

Ann Nathan Gallery, 33.
212 W Superior St ☎ 664-6622

Around the Coyote, 11.
1935 W North Ave ☎ 773/342-6777

Listed Alphabetically (cont.)

Carl Hammer Gallery, 23.
740 N Wells St ☎ 266-8512

Carrie Secrist Gallery, 54.
835 W Washington Ave ☎ 491-0917

Cassiopeia, 16.
433 N Wells ☎ 464-1111

Chicago Center for the Print, 5.
1509 W Fullerton Ave ☎ 773/477-1585

Contemporary Art Workshop, 7.
542 W Grant Pl ☎ 773/472-4004

David Leonardis Gallery, 47.
1346 N Paulina St ☎ 773/278-3058

David Weinberg Gallery, 13.
300 W Superior ☎ 529-5090

Donald Young Gallery, 53.
933 W Washington Blvd ☎ 455-0100

Douglas Dawson Gallery, 44.
400 N Morgan ☎ 226-7975

DVA, 4.
2568 N Lincoln Ave ☎ 773/871-4DVA

Eastern Gallery, 22.
750 N Franklin St ☎ 280-0787

Ferrari Sturdios, 17.
412 S Wells ☎ 922-2993

Flatfile Gallery, 47.
217 N Carpenter ☎ 491-1190

Galleries Maurice Sternberg, 20.
875 N Michigan Ave, Ste 2850
☎ 642-1700

Gallery 203, 11.
1579 N Milwaukee Ave
☎ 773/252-1952

Gallery 500 Wells, 31.
500 N Wells ☎ 222-1880

Gallery Stuart-Rodgers, 43.
375 W Erie ☎ 787-8696

Gescheidle, 48.
1039 W Lake St ☎ 226-3500

**The Green Lantern Gallery
and Press, 12.**
1511 N Milwaukee Ave
☎ 773/235-0936

G R N'Namdi Gallery, 52.
110 N Peoria St ☎ 563-9240

Gruen Galleries, 35.
226 W Superior St ☎ 337-6262

Habatat Galleries, 34.
222 W Superior St ☎ 440-0288

Havana Gallery, 5.
1139 W Webster Ave ☎ 773/549-2492

I space, 36.
230 W Superior St ☎ 587-9976

Jean Albano Gallery, 26.
215 W Superior ☎ 440-0770

Joel Oppenheimer, Inc., 18.
410 N Michigan Ave ☎ 642-5300

Joseph Glimer Gallery Ltd., 26.
207 W Superior ☎ 787-4640

Judy A Saslow Gallery, 37.
300 W Superior St ☎ 943-0530

Kass/Meridian, 41.
325 W Huron St ☎ 266-5999

Kavi Gupta Gallery, 54.
835 W Washington ☎ 432-0708

Las Manos, 1.
5220 N Clark St ☎ 773/728-8910

Lill Street Art Center, 2.
4401 N Ravenswood Ave
☎ 773/769-4226

Linda Warren Gallery, 45.
1052 W Fulton ☎ 432-9500

Lydon Fine Art, Inc., 40.
340 W Superior St ☎ 943-1133

Mars Gallery, 46.
1139 W Fulton ☎ 226-7808

Marx-Saunders Gallery, Ltd, 36.
230 W Superior St ☎ 573-1400

Mary Bell Gallery, 38.
740 N Franklin St ☎ 642-0202

Maya Polsky Gallery, 26.
215 W Superior St ☎ 440-0055

Melanee Cooper Gallery, 38.
740 N Franklin St ☎ 202-9305

Mi Elements, 58.
851 W Randolph ☎ 243-9711

Mongerson Galleries, 28.
704 N Wells St ☎ 943-2354

Monique Meloche, 50.
118 N Peoria ☎ 455-0299

Old Town Art Center, 8.
1763 N North Park Ave ☎ 337-1938

Orca Aart Gallery, 55.
651 W Washington St ☎ 463-1004

Packer Schopf Gallery, 49.
942 W Lake St ☎ 226-8984

Perimeter Gallery, 32.
210 W Superior St ☎ 266-9473

Peter Jones, 3.
1806 W Cuyler Ave ☎ 773/472-9723

Portals, Ltd., 24.
742 N Wells St ☎ 642-1066

Primitive, 56.
130 N Jefferson ☎ 575-9600

Printworks Gallery, 39.
311 W Superior St ☎ 664-9407

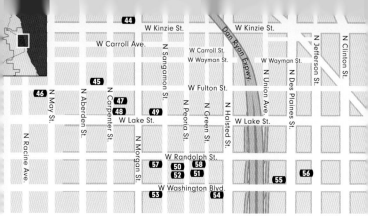

West Loop Detail Listed by Site Number

44 Douglas Dawson Gallery

45 Linda Warren Gallery

46 Mars Gallery

47 Flatfile Gallery

48 Gescheidle

49 Packer Schopf Gallery

50 Monique Meloche

50 Walsh Gallery

50 Rhona Hoffman

51 Tony Wight Gallery

52 GR N'Namdi

53 Donald Young Gallery

54 Carrie Secrist Gallery

54 Kavi Gupta Gallery

54 Thomas McCormick Gallery

55 Orca Art Gallery

56 Primitive

57 Thomas Robertello Gallery

58 Mi Elements Gallery

Listed Alphabetically

R H Love Galleries, 19.
645 N Michigan Ave ☎ 640-1300

R S Johnson Fine Art, 19.
645 N Michigan Ave ☎ 943-1661

Rhona Hoffman, 50.
118 N Peoria St ☎ 455-1990

Richard Gray Gallery, 20.
875 N Michigan Ave ☎ 642-8877

Richard Reed Armstrong Fine Art, 21. 200 E Walton St ☎ 664-9312

Robert Henry Adams Fine Art, 29.
715 N Franklin St ☎ 642-8700

Roy Boyd Gallery, 25.
739 N Wells St ☎ 642-1606

Schneider Gallery, 36.
230 W Superior St ☎ 988-4033

Spencer Weisz Galleries, Ltd, 14.
843 W Chicago ☎ 923-0910

Stephen Daiter Gallery, 39.
311 W Superior St ☎ 787-3350

Th!nk Art, 10.
1530 N Paulina ☎ 773/252-8672

Thomas Masters Gallery, 9.
245 W North Ave ☎ 440-2322

Thomas McCormick Gallery, 54.
835 W Washington Blvd
☎ 773/226-6800

Thomas Robertello Gallery, 57.
939 W Randolph ☎ 421-1587

Tony Wight Gallery, 51.
119 N Peoria St ☎ 492-7261

Vale Craft Gallery, 18.
230 W Superior St ☎ 337-3525

Walsh Gallery, 50.
118 N Peoria ☎ 829-3312

Zg Gallery, 37.
300 W Superior St ☎ 654-9900

Zolla/Lieberman Gallery, 41.
325 W Huron St ☎ 944-1990

Zygman Voss, 34.
222 W Superior St ☎ 787-3300

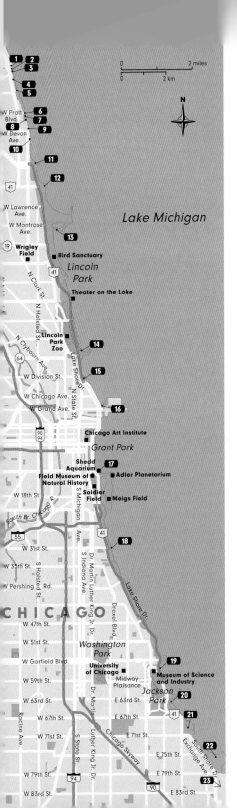

**Listed by
Site Number**

1 Juneway Beach

2 Rogers Beach

3 Howard Beach

4 Fargo Beach/Jarvis Beach

5 Leone Beach

6 Pratt Beach/Hartigan Beach

7 Columbia Ave Park & Beach

8 North Shore Beach

9 Albion Beach/Loyola Beach

10 Thorndale Beach

11 Osterman Beach

12 Foster Ave Beach

13 Montrose Beach

14 North Ave Beach

15 Oak St Beach

16 Ohio St Beach

17 12th St Beach

18 31st St Beach

19 57th St Beach

20 63rd St Beach

21 South Shore Cultural Center Beach

22 Rainbow Beach

23 Calumet Beach

Pottawattomie Park
Rogers Park
W Touhy Ave.
Lerner Park
ppewa Park
Rogers Ave. Park
Jarvis Ave. Park
Touhy Park
Indian Boundary Park
W Pratt Blvd.
Warren Park
W Devon Ave.
Green Briar Park
Peterson St.
Mather Park
ion rk
Senn Park
N Rogers St.
Loyola Park
Pratt Blvd. Park
Hartigan Park
Loyola U
Berger Park Lane Park

14

W Foster St.

41

River Park
Winnemac Park
N Lincoln Ave.
Welles Park
Horner Park
McFetridge Sports Center
W Addison Ave.
W Belmont Ave.
Hamlin Park
mer square
Holstein Park
Wicker Park
Pulaski Park
Clemente Park
Eckhart Park
W Chicago Ave.
Bickerdike Sq. Park
W Grand Ave.
Union Park
Washington Blvd.
W Madison St.
United Center
Garibaldi Park
Altgeld Park

Lincoln Park
W Lawrence Ave.
Clarendon Park
W Montrose Ave.
Chicago Corinthian Yacht Club
Waveland Golf Course
Wrigley Field
Bird Sanctuary
Chicago Yacht Club
Diversey Driving Range
Diversey Yacht Club
Nature Museum
Oz Park
Lincoln Park Zoo
Stanton Schiller Park
W Division St.
Seward Park
Washington Sq. Park
Lake Shore Park

Lake Michigan

Lincoln Park

Lake Shore Park
Olive Park
Navy Pier Park
Lake Shore East Park
Columbia Yacht Club/
Chicago Yacht Club
Millenium Park
Grant Park
Shedd Aquarium
Adler Planetarium
Burnham Harbor Yacht Club
Northerly Island

N

KEY
Beaches
Bike paths
Fishing
Golf Courses
Marinas
Swimming Pools
Tennis Courts

0   2 miles
0   2 km

19

64

N Western Ave.
mboldt Park
smith Park

90
94

Sheridan Park
Arrigo Park
UIC
Field Museum
Soldier Field
Ping Tour Memorial Park
Chicago Women's Park and Gardens

CHICAGO

Douglas Park
W 18th St.
Harrison Park
Cermak Rd.
S Blue Island Ave.
Addams Park
Dvorak Park
South Br.
Chicago Dr.

55

Williams Park
Dunbar Park
Lake Meadows Park
Groveland Park
Woodland Park

McGuane Park
W 31st St.
Armour Park
Hoyne Park
W 35th St.
McKinley Park
W Pershing Rd.
U.S. Cellular Field
Stateway Park

Ellis Park
Madden Park

Burnham Park

S Dr. Martin Luther King Jr. Dr.
S Indiana Ave.

Kelly Park
Davis Sq. Park
Cornell Sq. Park
W 47th St.
Fuller Park
Taylor Park

Hermitage Park
Sherwood Park
W 59th St.
Ogden Park
W 63rd St.

S California Ave.
W Garfield Blvd.
Sherman Park
Gage Park
Lindblom Park
arquette

Washington Park
University of Chicago
Nichols Park
Museum of Science and Industry
Midway Plaisance
Jackson Park
E 63rd St.
Jackson Park Yacht Club/
Shore Yacht Club
E 67th St.

Kenwood Park
Harold Washington Park

Drexel Blvd.
Lake Shore Dr.

South Shore Cultural Center
Rainbow Park
E 71st St.
Hodes Park
E 75th St.

94

90

Hamilton Park

S Western Ave.
S Ashland Ave.
Racine Ave.
S Halsted St.
S State St.
S Michigan Ave.
S Dr. Martin Luther King Jr. Dr.

W Hollywood Ave.

W Bryn Mawr Ave. 5600N

Bike Way
(18.5 miles from
Hollywood Ave. to 71st St.)

Foster Avenue Beach

Foster Beach House

5200N W Foster Ave.

Lincoln Park

W Argyle St.

W Ainslie St.

Margate Field House

4800N W Lawrence Ave.

W Leland Ave.

W Wilson Ave.

Clarendon Park Community Center Athletic Fields

Clarendon Park

4400N W Montrose Ave.

Montrose Beach

Montrose Beach House

W Montrose Dr.

Montrose Harbor

Graceland Cemetery

W Buena Ave.

Lake Michigan

800W

Sydney R. Marovitz
(Waveland)
Golf Course

4000N W Irving Park Rd.

W Sheridan Rd.

W Grace St.

Waveland Clock Tower

W Waveland Ave.

Bird Sanctuary

Wrigley Field

3600N W Addison St.

W Cornelia Ave.

Chicago Yacht Club

Lincoln Park

W Roscoe St.

W Aldine Ave.

Belmont Harbor

W Melrose St.

3200N W Belmont Ave.

W Wellington Ave.

Telcser Playlot

W Diversey Ave.

Diversey Driving Range

2800N

Diversey Harbor

Diversey Yacht Club

W Wrightwood Ave.

North Pond

Theatre on the Lake

W Altgeld St.

Peggy Notebaert Nature Museum

2400N W Fullerton Ave.

W Fullerton Pkwy.

W Belden Ave.

Conservatory

W Webster Ave.

Lincoln Park Zoo

W Dickens Ave.

2000N

Cummings Playlot

Lincoln Park

W Armitage Ave.

South Pond

Lincoln Park

North Avenue Beach

South Athletic Fields

North Avenue Beach House

Chicago History Museum

1600N W North Ave.

North Blvd.

N

1500 feet

500 meters

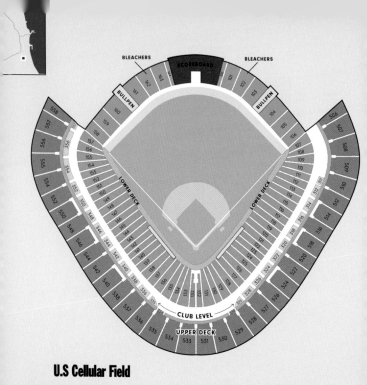

U.S Cellular Field

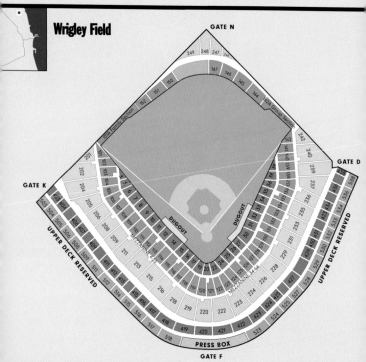

Wrigley Field

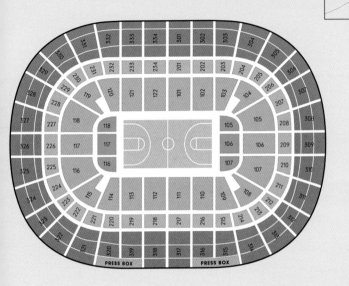

United Center

Soldier Field

Listed by Site Number
NEAR NORTH

1 Barbara's Bookstore
2 Newberry Library Bookstore
3 Ultimo
4 Tod's
5 Marina Rinaldi
6 Hermès
7 Elements
8 Jil Sander
9 MAC Cosmetics
10 Prada
11 Jake
12 Barneys New York
13 John Varvatos
14 Juicy Couture
14 Kate Spade
15 G'Bani
16 Yves Saint Laurent
17 Pratesi Linens
18 Chanel
19 Bloomingdales
19 900 N Michigan Avenue Shops
19 Mark Shale
20 Sur La Table
21 Diesel
22 Children in Paradise
23 Ikram
24 The North Face
24 Paul Stuart
25 Escada
26 H & M
27 American Girl Place
27 Macy's

27 Water Tower Place
28 Borders Books & Music
29 Giorgio Armani
30 Polo Ralph Lauren
31 Neiman Marcus
32 Tiffany & Co
33 Disney Store
34 Only She
35 Saks Fifth Avenue
36 Saks Fifth Avenue, Men's Store
37 Brooks Brothers
38 Apple
39 Cole Haan
40 NikeTown
41 Crate & Barrel
42 Ferragamo
42 Kenneth Cole
43 Burberry
44 Eddie Bauer
44 Original Levi's Store
44 Ann Taylor
45 Bloomingdales Home
46 Nordstrom
46 Shops at North Bridge
47 Jazz Record Mart
48 Pearl
49 Alcala's Western Wear
50 Luminaire
51 Michael FitzSimmons
52 Clever Alice
53 Sawbridge Studios

54 P.O.S.H
55 Rita Bucheit, Ltd
56 The Golden Triangle
57 Cambium
58 Jay Robert's Antique Warehouse

LOOP
59 Illinois Artisans Shop
60 Borders
61 Gallery 37
62 Loehman's
63 Brent Books
64 Syd Jerome
65 Block 37
66 Macy's
66 Fox & Obel
68 Iwan Ries & Co
69 H & M
70 Nordstrom Rack
70 Sears
71 Urban Outfitters
72 Blick Art Materials
73 Akira
74 Books A Million
75 Brooks Brothers
76 Symphony Store
77 Chicago Architecture Foundation
78 Central Camera
79 Utrecht
80 Prairie Avenue Bookshop
81 Florodora

Listed Alphabetically

NEAR NORTH

Alcala's Western Wear, 49.
1733 W Chicago Ave ☎ 226-0152.

American Girl Place, 22.
835 N Michigan Ave
☎ 877/247-5223.

Ann Taylor, 39. 600 N Michigan Ave
☎ 587-8301. Womenswear

Apple N Michigan Ave., 32
679 N Michigan Ave ☎ 981-4104.
Computers

Barbara's Bookstore, 1.
1350 N Wells St ☎ 642-5044

Barneys New York, 12.
25 E Oak St ☎ 587-1700. Clothing

Bloomingdales, 19.
900 N. Michigan Ave ☎ 440-4460.
Department Store

Bloomingdales Home & Furniture, 40.
600 N Wabash Ave ☎ 324-7500.

Borders Books & Music, 23.
830 N. Michigan Ave ☎ 573-0564

Brooks Brothers, 31.
713 N. Michigan Ave ☎ 915-0060.
Clothing

Burberry, 38.
633 N. Michigan Ave ☎ 787-2500.
Clothing

Cambium, 57.
119 W. Hubbard St ☎ 832-9920.
Home Furnishings

Chanel, 18. 935 N. Michigan Ave
☎ 787-5500. Womenswear

Children in Paradise, 17. 909 N Rush
St ☎ 951-5440. Children's Books

Clever Alice, 52. 750 N Franklin St
☎ 587-8693. Boutique

Cole Haan, 33. 673 N Michigan Ave
☎ 642-8995. Shoes

Crate & Barrel, 36. 646 N Michigan
Ave ☎ 787-5900. Housewares

Diesel, 16. 923 N Rush St
☎ 255-0157. Clothing

Disney Store, 45. 717 N Michigan Ave
☎ 654-9208. Toys

Eddie Bauer, 39. 600 N Michigan Ave
☎ 951-8484. Clothing

Elements, 7. 102 E Oak St ☎ 642-6574.
Home Furnishings

Escada, 21. 840 N Michigan Ave
☎ 915-0500. Womenswear

Ferragamo, 37. 645 N Michigan Ave
☎ 397-0464. Shoes

G'Bani, 35.
72 E Oak St ☎ 440-1718.
Boutique

Giorgio Armani, 24.
800 W Michigan Ave ☎ 573-4220.
Clothing

The Golden Triangle, 56.
330 N Clark St ☎ 755-1266.
Asian Antiques

H & M, 25. 840 N Michigan Ave
☎ 640-0060. Clothing

Hermès of Paris, 6. 110 E Oak St
☎ 787-8175. Clothing

Ikram, 41. 873 N Rush St ☎ 587-1000.
Clothing

Jake, 11. 939 N Rush St ☎ 664-5553.
Boutique

**Jay Robert's Antique Warehouse,
58.** 149 W Kinzie St ☎ 222-0167

Jazz Record Mart, 46.
27 E Illinois St ☎ 222-1467

Jil Sander, 8. 48 E Oak St
☎ 335-0006. Womenswear

John Varvatos, 14. 930 N Rush St
(opens fall 2009). Menswear

Juicy Couture, 13. 101 E Oak St
☎ 280-1637. Clothing

Kate Spade, 13. 101 E Oak St
☎ 654-8853. Accessories

Kenneth Cole, 42. 540 N Michigan Ave
☎ 644-1163. Clothing/Shoes

Luminaire, 50. 301 W Superior St
☎ 664-9582. Furniture

MAC Cosmetics, 9. 40 E Oak St
☎ 951-7310

Macy's, 22. 835 N Michigan Ave
☎ 335-7700. Department Store

Marina Rinaldi, 5. 113 E Oak St
☎ 867-8700. Full-Figured Womanswear

Mark Shale, 19. 900 N Michigan Ave
☎ 440-0721. Clothing

**Michael FitzSimmons Decorative
Arts, 51.** 311 W Superior St
☎ 787-0496. Antiques

Neiman Marcus, 27. 737 N Michigan
Ave ☎ 642-5900. Department Store

Newberry Library Bookstore, 2.
60 W Walton St ☎ 255-3520.

NikeTown, 34.
669 N Michigan Ave ☎ 642-6363.
Sporting Goods

900 N Michigan Ave Shops, 19.
☎ 915-3916. Shopping Center

Listed Alphabetically

Nordstrom, 43.
55 E Grand Ave
☎ 464–1515. Department Store

The North Face, 20.
875 N Michigan Ave ☎ 337–7200.
Outdoor Clothing/Gear

Only She, 54. 710 N State St
☎ 335–1353. Boutique

Original Levi's Store, 39.
600 N Michigan Ave ☎ 642–9613. Jeans

Paul Stuart, 20.
875 N Michigan Ave ☎ 640–2650.
Menswear

Pearl, 48.
225 W Chicago Ave
☎ 915–0200. Art Supplies

Polo Ralph Lauren, 26.
750 N Michigan Ave ☎ 280–1655.
Clothing/Home

P.O.S.H, 54.
613 N State St ☎ 280–1602. China

Prada, 10. 30 Oak St ☎ 951–1113.
Clothing

Pratesi Linens, 44.
67 E Oak St ☎ 943–8422. Linens

Rita Bucheit, Ltd, 55.
449 N Wells ☎ 527–4080. Antiques

Saks Fifth Avenue, 30.
700 N Michigan Ave ☎ 944–6500.
Department Store

Saks Fifth Avenue, Men's Store, 29.
717 N Michigan Ave ☎ 944–6500.

Sawbridge Studios, 53.
153 W Ohio St ☎ 828–0055.
Furniture/Home

Shops at North Bridge, 43.
520 N Michigan Ave ☎ 327–2300.
Shopping Center

Sur La Table, 15.
52–54 E Walton St ☎ 337–0600.
Kitchen

Tiffany & Co., 28.
730 N Michigan Ave ☎ 944–7500.
Jewelery

Tod's, 4.
121 E Oak St ☎ 943–0070. Shoes

Ultimo, 3.
114 E Oak St ☎ 787–1171.
Womenswear

Water Tower Place, 22.
835 N Michigan Ave ☎ 440–3166.
Shopping Center

Yves Saint Laurent, 42.
51 E Oak St ☎ 751–8995. Clothing

LOOP

Akira, 78. 122 S State St ☎ 346–3034.
Shoes

Blick Art Materials, 72. 42 S State St
☎ 920–0300. Art Supplies

Block 37, 65. 108 N State St (opens May
2009). Shopping Center

Books A Million, 74. 144 S Clark St
☎ 857–0613

Borders Books & Music, 60.
150 N State St ☎ 606–0750.

Brent Books, 63.
309 W Washington Blvd ☎ 364–0126.

Brooks Brothers, 75. 209 S LaSalle St
☎ 263–0100. Menswear

Central Camera, 78.
230 S Wabash Ave ☎ 427–5580

Chicago Architecture Foundation, 77.
224 S Michigan Ave ☎ 922–3432.
Architecture Books/Crafts

Florodora, 81. 330 S Dearborn St
☎ 212–8860. Boutique

Fox & Obel, 68. 1 S State St (opens fall
20009). Gourmet Groceries/Foods

Gallery 37, 61. 66 E Randolph St
☎ 744–7274. Crafts

H & M, 69.
22 State St ☎ 263–3614. Clothing

Illinois Artisans Shop, 59.
100 W Randolph St ☎ 814–5321. Crafts

Iwan Ries & Co, 67.
19 S Wabash Ave ☎ 372–1306.
Cigars/Pipes

Loehman's, 62. 151 N State St
☎ 705–3810. Clothing

Macy's, 66. 111 N State St
☎ 781–1000. Department Store

Nordstrom Rack, 70. 24 N State St
☎ 377–5500. Clothing/Shoes

Prairie Avenue Bookshop, 80.
418 S Wabash Ave
☎ 922–8311. Architecture Books

Sears, 70. 2 N State St ☎ 373–6096.
Department Store

The Symphony Store, 76.
220 S Michigan Ave ☎ 294–3345.
Music/Gifts

Syd Jerome, 64. 2 N LaSalle St
☎ 346–0333. Menswear

Urban Outfitter's, 71. 20 S State St
☎ 269–9919. Clothing/Home Decor

Utrecht, 79. 332 S Michigan Ave
☎ 922–7565. Art Supplies

Listed by Site Number

1 Lulu's at the Belle Kay
2 Jake
3 Judith Racht
4 The Good Olde Days
5 Uncle Fun
6 Chicago Antique Center
7 Bittersweet
8 Windward Sports
9 Unabridged Bookstore
10 Reckless Records
11 Threadless
12 Tragically Hip
13 Borders Books and Music
14 Barnes & Noble
15 Powell's Bookstore
16 Barnes & Noble
17 Robin Richman
18 G-Boutique

19 Kachibachi
20 Virtu
21 Green City Market
22 Running Away
23 Stitch
24 Barneys Co-op
25 Cynthia Rowley
26 Lori's
27 Aroma Workshop
28 Little Strummer
29 Paper Source
30 Active Endeavors
31 Art Effect
32 B Boutique
33 Tabula Tua
34 Jayson Home and Garden
35 CB2
36 Marc Jacobs
37 Clothes Minded
38 P. 45
39 Quimby's

40 TK Men
41 City Soles/Niche
42 John Fluevog
43 Brooklyn Industries
44 Hejfina
45 Akira
46 Futurgarb
47 Maria Pinto
48 The Oprah Store
49 2 Sisters

Listed Alphabetically

2 Sisters, 49. 1167 W Madison St
☎ 226-6677. Clothing

Active Endeavors, 30.
835 W Armitage Ave ☎ 773/281-8100.
Sporting Goods/Clothes

Akira, 45. 1837 W North Ave
☎ 773/489-0818. Clothing

Aroma Workshop, 27.
2050 N. Halsted St
☎ 773/871-1985. Scent

Art Effect, 31. 934 W Armitage Ave
☎ 929-3600. Womenswear

B Boutique, 32. 1117 W Armitage Ave
☎ 773/665-1102. Womenswear

Barnes & Noble Booksellers, 14.
659 W Diversey Ave ☎ 773/871-9004.

Barnes & Noble Booksellers, 16.
1441 W Webster Ave ☎ 773/871-3610

Barneys Co-op, 24. 2209 N Halstead
St ☎ 773/248-0426. Clothing

Bittersweet, 7. 1114 W Belmont Ave
☎ 773/929-1100. Bakery

Borders Books and Music, 13.
2817 N Clark St ☎ 773/935-3909

Brooklyn Industries, 43.
1426 N Milwaukee Ave
☎ 773/360-8182. Clothing

CB2, 35. 800 W North Ave
☎ 787-8329. Furniture/Home Decor

Chicago Antique Centre, 6.
3036 N Lincoln Ave ☎ 773/929-0200.

City Soles/Niche, 41. 2001 W North
Ave ☎ 773/489-2001. Shoes

Clothes Minded, 37. 1735 N Damen
Ave ☎ 773/227-3402. Clothing

Cynthia Rowley, 25.
808 W Armitage Ave
☎ 773/528-6160. Womenswear

Futurgarb, 46. 1359 N Milwaukee Ave
☎ 773/276-1450. Boutique

G-Boutique, 18. 2131 N Damen Ave
☎ 773/235-1234. Lingerie/Sex Toys

The Good Olde Days, 4.
2138 W Belmont Ave
☎ 773/472-8837. Antiques

Green City Market, 21. 1750 N Clark
St ☎ 773/880-1266. Organic Produce

Hejfina, 44. 1529 N Milwaukee Ave
☎ 773/772-0002. Clothing/
Home Decor

Jake, 2. 3740 N Southport Ave
☎ 773/929-5253. Boutique

Jayson Home and Garden, 34.
1885 N Clybourn Ave ☎ 773/248-8180.

John Fluevog, 42.
1539 N Milwaukee Ave
☎ 773/772-1983. Shoes

Judith Racht Gallery, 3.
3727 N Southport Ave
☎ 773/281-3705. Folk Art

Kachibachi, 1. 2041 N Damen Ave
†773/645-8640. Home

Little Strummer, 28. 909 W Armitage
Ave ☎ 773/751-3410. Kids/Music

Lori's, 26. 824 W Armitage Ave
☎ 773/281-5655. Shoes

Lulu's at the Belle Kay, 1.
3862 N Lincoln Ave
☎ 773/404-5858. Vintage Clothes

Marc Jacobs, 36. 1714 Damen Ave
☎ 773/276-1698. Clothing

Maria Pinto, 47. 135 N Jefferson St
☎ 773/648-1335. Clothing

The Oprah Store, 48. 37 N Carpenter
St ☎ 773/633-2100. Eclectic

P. 45, 38. 1643 N Damen Ave
☎ 773/862-4523. Womenswear

Paper Source, 29.
919 W Armitage Ave ☎ 773/525-7300.

Powell's Bookstore, 15.
2850 N Lincoln Ave ☎ 773/248-1444.

Quimby's, 39. 1854 W North Ave
☎ 773/342-0910. Zines/Comics/Books

Reckless Records, 10.
3157 N Broadway ☎ 773/404-5080.

Robin Richman, 17. 2108 N Damen Ave
☎ 773/278-6150

Running Away, 41. 1753 N Damen Ave
☎ 773/395-AWAY. Sporting Goods

Stitch, 23. 1723 N Damen Ave
☎ 773/782-1570. Home/Bags

TK Men, 40. 1909 W North Ave
☎ 773/342-9800. Menswear

Tabula Tua, 33. 1015 W Armitage Ave
☎ 773/525-3500. Tableware

Threadless, 11. 3011 N Broadway
☎ 773/525-8640. T-Shirts

Tragically Hip, 12. 914 W Belmont Ave
☎ 773/549-1500. Boutique

Unabridged Bookstore, 9.
3251 N Broadway ☎ 773/883-9119

Uncle Fun, 5. 1338 W Belmont Ave
☎ 773/477-8223. Toys

Virtu, 20. 2034 N Damen Ave
☎ 773/235-3790. Crafts

Windward Sports, 8.
3317 N Clark St ☎ 773/472-6868.
Skate-/Snowboarding

Listed by Site Number

1 The Palm	**8** Wishbone	**15** Meiji
2 Aria	**9** Sushi Wabi	**16** Blackbird
3 Catch 35	**10** Vivo	**17** Avec
4 Nine	**11** Red Light	**18** Rivers
5 Follia	**12** Marché	**19** Atwood Cafe
6 Moto	**13** Ina's	**20** Trattoria No. 10
7 La Sardine	**14** one sixtyblue	**21** Nick's Fishmarket

Listed Alphabetically

Aria, 2. 200 N Columbus Dr
☎ 444-9494. American. $$$

Atwood Cafe, 19. 1 W Washington Blvd
☎ 368-1900. American. $$-$$$

Avec, 17. 615 W Randolph St
☎ 377-2002. Mediterranean. $$$

The Berghoff, 24. 17 W Adams St
☎ 427-3170. German. $-$$

Blackbird, 16. 619 W Randolph St
☎ 715-0708. New American. $$$

Catch 35, 3. 35 W Wacker Dr
☎ 346-3500. Seafood. $$$

Chez Joel, 32. 1119 W Taylor St
☎ 226-6479. French. $$-$$$

Chicago Firehouse Restaurant, 35.
1401 S Michigan Ave ☎ 786-1401.
American. $$$

Costa's, 30. 340 S Halsted St
☎ 263-9700. Greek. $-$$$

Custom House, 26. 500 S Dearborn
St ☎ 523-0200. New American. $$$

Everest, 27. 440 S LaSalle St
☎ 663-8920. French. $$$$

Follia, 5. 953 W Fulton Market
☎ 243-2888. Italian. $$-$$$

Francesca's on Taylor, 34.
1400 W Taylor St ☎ 829-2828.
Italian. $$$

Ina's, 13. 1235 W Randolph St
☎ 226-8227. American. $$

La Sardine, 7. 111 N Carpenter St
☎ 421-2800. Bistro. $$-$$$

Lou Mitchell's, 28. 565 W Jackson St
☎ 939-3111. Breakfast. $

Marché, 13. 833 W Randolph St
☎ 226-8399. French. $$-$$$$

Meiji, 15. 623 W Randolph St
☎ 887-9999. Sushi. $$$

Moto, 6.
945 W Fulton St ☎ 491-0058.
Asian. $$$$

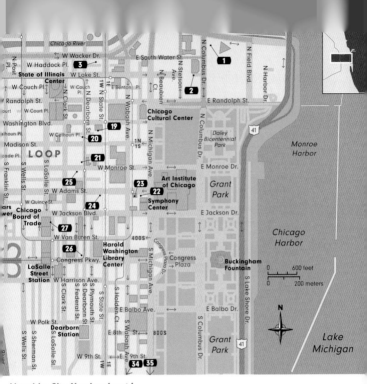

Listed by Site Number (cont.)

22 Russian Tea
   Time
23 Rhapsody
24 The Berghoff
25 Vivere
26 Custom House
27 Everest

28 Lou Mitchell's
29 Parthenon
30 Costa's
31 Tuscany
32 Chez Joel
33 Francesca's
   on Taylor

34 Opera
35 Chicago Firehouse

Nick's Fishmarket, 21.
51 S Clark St ☎ 621-0200.
Seafood. $$$-$$$$

Nine, 4. 440 W Randolph St
☎ 575-9900. American. $$$$

one sixtyblue, 14. 160 N Loomis St
☎ 850-0303. New American. $$$

Opera, 34. 1301 S Wabash Ave
☎ 461-0161. Pan-Asian. $$$

The Palm, 1. 323 E Wacker Dr
☎ 616-1000. Steakhouse. $$$$

Parthenon, 29. 314 S Halsted St
☎ 726-2407. Greek. $-$$

Red Light, 11. 820 W Randolph St
☎ 733-8880. Pan-Asian. $$$

Rhapsody, 23. 65 E Adams St
☎ 786-9911. New American. $$$

Rivers, 18. 30 S Wacker Dr
☎ 559-1515. American. $$$

Russian Tea Time, 22. 77 E Adams St
☎ 360-0000. Russian. $$$

Sushi Wabi, 9. 842 W Randolph St
☎ 563-1224. Sushi. $$$

Trattoria No. 10, 20. 10 N Dearborn St
☎ 984-1718. Italian. $$$

Tuscany, 31. 1014 W Taylor St
☎ 829-1990. Italian. $$$

Vivere, 25. 71 W Monroe St
☎ 332-4040. Italian. $$-$$$

Vivo, 10. 838 W Randolph St
☎ 733-3379. Italian.$$$

Wishbone, 8. 1001 W Washington Blvd
☎ 850-2663. Southern. $

$$$$ = over $28 $$$ = $21-$28 $$ = $15-$20 $ = under $15
Per person, for a main course at dinner.

OLD TOWN

W Germania Pl.

W Burton Pl.　W Burton Pl.　E Burton Pl.

N Sedgwick St.　N Orleans St.　N Park St.　N Wieland St.　N Wells St.

W Schiller St.

N LaSalle St.　N Clark St.　N Dearborn St.　N State Pkwy　N Astor St.

E Schiller St.

N Cleveland St.　N Hudson St.

W Sullivan St.　W Evergreen St.

Schick Pl.

W Goethe St.　W Goethe St.

N Astor St.　N Banks Ct.　Ritchie

E Goethe St.

W Scott St.　E Scott St.

W Division St.　1200N　W Division St.　E Division St.

Seward Park

W Elm St.

W Elm St.

GOL
COAS

W Hill St.　W Maple St.

E Cedar St.

W Hobbie St.

E Bellevue Pl.

W Wendell St.

E Oak St.

W Oak St.　W Oak St.

N Rush St.

W Walton St.

E Walton St.

W Locust St.

Washington Square

W Delaware St.　E Delaware P

N Wells St.

W Delaware St.

N Hudson Ave.

W Chestnut St.

E Chestnut St.

W Chestnut St.

N State St.

E Pearson St.

W Institute Pl.

RIVER NORTH

W Chicago Ave.　800N　W Chicago Ave.　E Chicago Ave.

W Superior St.

Clark St.

N Hudson Ave.　N Sedgwick St.　N Orleans St.　N Franklin St.

W Huron St.

NEAR NORTH

Dearborn St.　State St.　Wabash Ave.

W Erie St.

W Ontario St.

400W

W Ohio St.

W Grand Ave.

N Kingsbury St.

W Illinois St.

W Hubbard St.

W Kinzie St.　400N

Wrigley Building

Chicago River

Listed by Site Number

1 Topo Gigio
2 Bistrot Margot
3 Fireplace Inn
4 Kamehachi
5 Twin Anchors
6 The Pump Room
7 Table Fifty-Two
8 Tsunami
9 ¡Salpicón!
10 Morton's of Chicago
11 Big Bowl
12 Gibson's
13 Le Colonial
14 Spiaggia
15 Seasons
16 McCormick & Schmick's
17 Mike Ditka's Restaurant
18 Signature Room at the 95th
18 Cheesecake Factory
19 Ritz-Carlton Dining Room
20 NoMI
21 Bistro 110
22 RL
23 Kiki's Bistro
24 MK
25 Zealous
26 Scoozi!
27 Nacional 27
28 Graham Elliot
29 Wildfire
30 Fogo de Chão
31 Ed Debevic's
32 Café Iberico
33 Zed451
34 Le Lan
35 Avenues
36 Shanghai Terrace
37 Roy's
38 Japonais
39 Wave
40 Les Nomades
41 Tru
42 Billy Goat Tavern
43 Joe's Be-Bop Café & Jazz Emporium
44 Riva
45 Fox & Obel Café
46 Caliterra
46 Capital Grille
47 Sayat Nova

Listed by Site Number (cont.)

48 Joe's Seafood
49 Heaven on Seven on Rush
50 Pizzeria Due
51 Pizzeria Uno
52 Quartino
53 Osteria Via Stato
54 Hard Rock Cafe
55 Rainforest Cafe
56 Crofton on Wells
57 Cyrano's Bistrot & Wine Bar
58 Tizi Melloul
59 Gene & Georgetti

60 Coco Pazzo
61 Klay Oven
62 Vermilion
63 Maggiano's Little Italy
64 Naha
65 Blue Water Grill
66 Ben Pao
67 Vong's Thai Kitchen
68 Shaw's Crab House & Blue Crab Lounge
69 Phil Stefani's
70 Keefer's
71 Sixteen

72 Ruth's Chris Steak House
73 Frontera Grill/ Topolobampo
74 Mambo Grill
75 Brasserie Jo
76 Harry Caray's
77 Bin 36
78 Smith & Wollensky

Listed Alphabetically

Aigre Doux, 62. 230 W Kinzie St
☎ 329-9400. French. $$$

Avenues, 35. 108 E Superior St
☎ 573-6754. Contemporary.
$$$-$$$$

Ben Pao, 66. 52 W Illinois St
☎ 222-1888. Chinese. $-$$

Big Bowl, 11. 6 E Cedar St
☎ 640-8888. Pan-Asian. $

Billy Goat Tavern, 42.
430 N Michigan Ave ☎ 222-1525.
Burgers. $

Bin 36, 77. 339 N Dearborn St
☎ 755-9463. Contemporary. $$-$$$

Bistrot Margot, 2. 1437 N Wells St
☎ 587-3660. Bistro. $$

Bistro 110, 21. 110 E Pearson St
☎ 266-3110. French. $$-$$$$

Blue Water Grill, 65.
520 N Dearborn St ☎ 777-1400.
Seafood/Sushi. $$$

Brasserie Jo, 75. 59 W Hubbard St
☎ 595-0800. French. $$-$$$

Café Iberico, 32. 739 N LaSalle St
☎ 573-1510. Tapas. $

Caliterra, 46. 633 N St Clair St
☎ 274-4444. Italian. $$-$$$$

Capital Grille, 46. 633 N St Clair St
☎ 337-9400. Steakhouse. $$$-$$$$

Cheesecake Factory, 18.
875 N Michigan Ave ☎ 337-1101.
American. $$

Coco Pazzo, 60. 300 W Hubbard St
☎ 836-0900. Italian. $$$$

Crofton on Wells, 56. 535 N Wells St
☎ 755-1790. New American. $$$$

Cyrano's Bistrot & Wine Bar, 57.
546 N Wells St ☎ 467-0546. French. $$

Ed Debevic's, 31. 640 N Wells St
☎ 664-1707. 50s Diner. $

Fireplace Inn, 3. 1448 N Wells St
☎ 664-5264. Barbecue. $-$$$

Fogo de Chão, 30. 661 N LaSalle St
☎ 932-9330. Churrascaria. $$$$

Fox & Obel Café, 45. 401 E Illinois St
☎ 379-0112. American. $

Frontera Grill/Topolobampo, 73.
445 N Clark St ☎ 661-1434.
Mexican. $$$

Gene & Georgetti, 59.
500 N Franklin St ☎ 527-3718.
Steakhouse. $$$$

Gibson's, 12. 1028 N Rush St
☎ 266-8999. Steakhouse. $$$$

Graham Elliot, 28.
217 W Huron St ☎ 624-9975.
New American. $$-$$$

Hard Rock Cafe, 54. 63 W Ontario St
☎ 943-2252. American. $-$$

Harry Caray's, 76. 33 W Kinzie St
☎ 828-0966. Italian/Steak. $$-$$$

Heaven on Seven on Rush, 49.
600 N Michigan Ave ☎ 280-7774.
Cajun/Creole. $

Japonais, 38. 600 W Chicago Ave
☎ 822-9600. Fusion. $$$

Joe's Be-Bop Café & Jazz Emporium, 43. Navy Pier,
600 E Grand Ave ☎ 595-5299.
Barbecue.-$$

Joe's Seafood, Prime Steaks & Stone Crab, 48.
60 E Grand St ☎ 379-5637.
Barbecue. $$$

Kamehachi, 4. 1400 N Wells St
☎ 664-3663. Japanese. $$$

Keefer's, 70. 20 W Kinzie St
☎ 467-9525. Steak. $$$$

Kiki's Bistro, 23. 900 N Franklin St
☎ 335-5454. French. $$-$$$

Listed Alphabetically (cont.)

Klay Oven, 61. 414 N Orleans St
☎ 527-3999. Indian. $–$$

Le Colonial, 13. 937 N Rush St
☎ 255-0088. Vietnamese. $$$

Le Lan, 34. 749 N Clark St
☎ 280-9100. French/Vietnamese. $$$

Les Nomades, 40. 222 E Ontario St
☎ 649-9010. French. $$$$

Maggiano's Little Italy, 63. 516 N
Clark St ☎ 644-7700. Italian. $$

Mambo Grill, 74. 412 N Clark St
☎ 467-9797. Pan-Latin. $–$$

McCormick & Schmick's, 16.
41 E Chestnut St ☎ 397-9500.
Seafood. $$

MK, 24. 868 N Franklin St
☎ 482-9179. Contemporary. $$–$$$

Mike Ditka's Restaurant, 17.
100 E Chestnut St ☎ 587-8989.
American/Steak. $$$

Morton's of Chicago, 10.
1050 N State St ☎ 266-4820.
Steakhouse. $$$–$$$$

Nacional 27, 27. 325 W Huron St
☎ 664-2727. Latin. $$

Naha, 64. 500 N Clark St
☎ 321-6242. Contemporary. $$–$$$$

NoMI, 20. 800 N Michigan Ave
☎ 239-4030. French. $$$$

Osteria Via Stato, 53. 620 N State St
☎ 642-8450. Italian. $$$$

Phil Stefani's, 69. 437 N Rush St
☎ 222-0101. Italian/Steak. $$$

Pizzeria Due, 50. 619 N Wabash Ave
☎ 943-2400. Pizza. $

Pizzeria Uno, 51. 29 E Ohio St
☎ 321-1000. Pizza. $

The Pump Room, 6. 1301 N State Pkwy
☎ 266-0360. American. $$$$

Quartino, 52 . 626 N State St
☎ 698-5000. Italian. $$

Rainforest Cafe, 55. 605 N Clark St
☎ 787-1501. American. $–$$

**Ritz Carlton Café and
Dining Room, 19.**
160 E Pearson St ☎ 573-5223.
French. $$$–$$$$

Riva, 44. Navy Pier,
700 E Grand Ave ☎ 644-7482.
Seafood. $$–$$$$

RL, 22. 115 E Chicago Ave
☎ 475-1100. American. $–$$$

Roy's, 37. 720 N State St
☎ 787-7599. Hawaiian. $$$

Ruth's Chris Steak House, 72.
431 N Dearborn St ☎ 321-1365.
Steakhouse. $$$$

!Salpicòn!, 9. 1252 N Wells St
☎ 988-7811. Mexican. $$–$$$

Sayat Nova, 47. 157 E Ohio St
☎ 644-9159. Middle Eastern. $$

Scoozi!, 26. 410 W Huron St
☎ 943-5900. Italian. $–$$$

Seasons, 15. 120 E Delaware Pl
☎ 649-2349. New American. $$$$

Shanghai Terrace, 36.
108 E Superior St ☎ 573-6695.
Chinese. $$$

**Shaw's Crab House & Blue Crab
Lounge, 68.** 21 E Hubbard St
☎ 527-2722. Seafood. $$$

Signature Room at the 95th, 18.
875 N Michigan Ave ☎ 787-9596.
American. $$$$

Sixteen, 71. 401 N Wabash Ave
☎ 588-8030. American. $$$$

Smith & Wollensky, 78. 318 N State St
☎ 670-9900. Steakhouse. $$$–$$$$

Spiaggia, 14. 980 N Michigan Ave
☎ 280-2750. Italian. $$$$

Table Fifty-Two, 7 52 W Elm St
☎ 573-4000. American Southern. $$$

Tizi Melloul, 58. 531 N Wells St
☎ 670-4338. Moroccan. $$–$$$

Topo Gigio, 1. 1516 N Wells St
☎ 266-9355. Italian. $$

Tru, 41. 676 N St Clair St
☎ 202-0001. Contemporary. $$$$

Tsunami, 8. 1160 N Dearborn Ave
☎ 642-9911. Japanese. $$–$$$$

Twin Anchors, 5. 1655 N Sedgewick
☎ 266-1616. American. $

Vermillion, 62. 10 W Hubbard St
☎ 527-4060. Latin/Indian. $$–$$$

Vong's Thai Kitchen, 67.
6 W Hubbard St ☎ 644-8664.
Thai. $–$$

Wave, 39. 644 N Lake Shore Dr
☎ 255-4460. Mediterranean. $$–$$$

Wildfire, 29. 159 W Erie St
☎ 787-9000. Steak. $$–$$$

Zealous, 25. 419 W Superior St
☎ 475-9112. Contemporary. $$$–$$$$

Zed451, 33. 739 N Clark St
☎ 888/493-3451. American. $$$

$$$$ = *over $28* $$$ = *$21–$28* $$ = *$15–$20* $ = *under $15*

Per person, for a main course at dinner.

Loyola U
6400N

Devon Ave.
WEST
ROGERS PARK
Granville Ave.
Granville Ave.
ROGERS PARK

Hollywood Park
6000N

NORTH PARK
Peterson Ave.
EDGEWAT

North Shore Channel
Lincoln Ave.
Bryn Mawr Ave.
Rosehill Cemetery
5600N
Bryn Mawr Ave.

Bowmanville Ave.
Balmoral Ave.
Damen Ave.
Ashland Ave.
Broadway
Sheridan Ave.
Balmoral Ave.

Virginia Ave.
Kedzie Ave.
Foster Ave.
5200N
Winnemac Park
Leavitt St.
Argyle St.

West River Park
East River Park
St. Boniface Cemetery

ALBANY PARK
3600W
3200W
Manor Ave.

Lawrence Ave.
4800N
UPTOWN

Virginia Ave.
Wilson Ave.
RAVENS-WOOD
Clark St.
Wilson Ave.
Broadway
Sheridan Ave.

Montrose Ave.
Welles Park
Lincoln Ave.
2000W
Montrose Ave.
Graceland Cemetery

IRVING PARK
Kimball Ave.
Berteau Ave.
Horner Park
2800W
2400W
Berteau Ave.
1600W

Central Park Ave.
Kedzie Ave.
Sacramento Ave.
California Ave.
Irving Park Rd.
4000N
1200W

Grace St.
NORTH CENTER
Grace St.
Wrigley Field

Addison St.
3600N

AVONDALE
Western Ave.
Damen Ave.
Roscoe St.
LAKEVIE

Hamlin Park
24
3200N
Belmont Ave.
Racine Ave.

Elston Ave.
Wellington Ave.

LOGAN SQUARE
N. Branch Chicago R.
2800N
Diversey Ave.
Lincoln

Logan Sq.
Rockwell St.
Lincoln

Fullerton Ave.
Humboldt Blvd.
Milwaukee Ave.
2400N
Fullerton Ave.
Racine
DePau

Palmer St.
Palmer Sq.
BUCK-TOWN
Clybourn Ave.
DEPAU

Wabansia Ave.
3600W
3200W
2800W
2400W
Damen Ave.
Leavitt St.

Homan Ave.
Kedzie Ave.
Cortland St.
Armitage Ave.

Humboldt Park
North Ave.
Wicker Park
UKRAINIAN VILLAGE
160

Hirsch St.
Rockwell St.
Western Ave.

Division St.
2000W
1600W
120

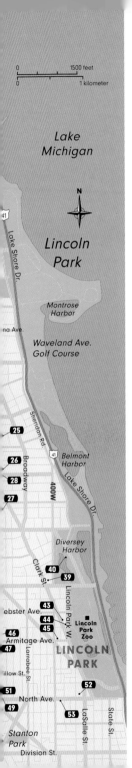

Listed Alphabetically
NORTH SIDE

Adobo Grill, 52. 1610 N Wells St ☎ 266-7999. Mexican. $$

Alinea, 50.
1723 N Halsted St ☎ 867-0110. American Contemporary. $$$$

Andies, 9. 5253 N Clark St ☎ 773/784-8616. Mediterranean. $

Ann Sather, 10. 5207 N Clark St ☎ 773/271-6677. Swedish/Breakfast $

Ann Sather, 31. 909 W Belmont Ave ☎ 773/348-2378. Swedish/Breakfast $

Arco de Cuchilleros, 25. 3445 N Halsted St ☎ 773/296-6046. Tapas. $$$

Arun's, 16. 4156 N Kedzie Ave ☎ 773/539-1909. Thai. $$$$

Bistro Campagne, 13. 4518 N Lincoln Ave ☎ 773/271-6100. French. $$

Boka, 48.
1729 N Halsted St ☎ 337-6070. American Contemporary. $$$

Bull-eh-Dia's Tapas Bar, 21. 3651 N Southport Ave ☎ 773/404-2855. Tapas. $

Buona Terra, 54.
2535 N California ☎ 773/289-3800. Italian. $

Cafe Ba-Ba-Reeba!, 46.
2024 N Halsted St ☎ 773/935-5000. Tapas. $$

Café 28, 18. 1800 W Irving Park Rd ☎ 773/528-2883. Latin. $$

Chalkboard, 15. 4343 N Lincoln Ave ☎ 773/477-7144. New American. $$$

Charlie Trotter's, 47.
816 W Armitage Ave ☎ 773/248-6228. New American. $$$$

Chicago Pizza &
Oven Grinder Co., 43. 2121 N Clark St ☎ 773/248-2570. Pizza. $

Coobah, 32. 3423 N Southport Ave ☎ 773/528-2220. Cuban. $$-$$$

Dee's, 42. 1114 W Armitage Ave ☎ 773/477-1500. Chinese. $

Deleece, 17. 4004 N Southport Ave ☎ 773/325-1710.
American Contemporary. $$-$$$

Erwin, 27. 2925 N Halsted St. ☎ 773/528-7200. American. $$-$$$

Flat Top Grill, 53. 319 W North Ave ☎ 787-7676. Stir Fry. $

Geja's Café, 45. 340 W Armitage Ave ☎ 773/281-9101. Fondue. $$$-$$$$

Green Dolphin Street, 55.
2200 N Ashland Ave ☎ 395-0066. American/International. $$$-$$$$

Heartland Café, 1.
7000 N Glenwood Ave ☎ 773/465-8005.
American/Vegetarian. $

Hema's Kitchen II, 39.
2411 N Clark St ☎ 773/529-1705. Indian. $

Hopleaf, 6. 5148 N Clark St ☎ 773/334-9851. Belgian. $$

Indian Garden, 2. 254 W Devon Ave ☎ 773/338-2929. Indian. $$-$$$

La Bocca della Verità, 12.
4618 N Lincoln Ave ☎ 773/784-6222. Italian. $$

La Donna, 11. 5146 N Clark St ☎ 773/561-9400. Italian. $-$$

La Tache, 8. 1475 W Balmoral Ave ☎ 773/334-7168. French Bistro. $$-$$$

Landmark, 49.
1633 N Halsted St ☎ 587-1600. American Contemporary. $$-$$$

Little Bucharest, 37. 3661 N Elston Ave ☎ 773/929-8640. Romanian. $

Lou Malnati Pizzeria, 38.
958 W Wrightwood Ave ☎ 773/832-4030. Pizza. $

Lula Café, 36.
2537 N Kedzie Blvd. ☎ 773/489-9554. American Contemporary. $-$$$

Lutnia, 35. 5532 W Belmont Ave ☎ 773/282-5335. Polish. $-$$$

Mama Desta's Red Sea, 30.
3216 N Clark St ☎ 773/935-7561. Ethiopian. $

Marigold, 19. 4832 N Broadway ☎ 773/293-4653. Indian. $$

Matsuya, 20. 3469 N Clark St ☎ 773/248-2677. Japanese. $

Mia Francesca, 29. 3311 N Clark St ☎ 773/281-3310. Italian. $$-$$$

Mon Ami Gabi, 41.
2300 N Lincoln Park W ☎ 773/348-8886. French. $$-$$$

North Pond, 40. 2610 N Cannon Dr ☎ 773/477-5845. American. $$$-$$$$

Orange, 28. 3231 N Clark St ☎ 773/549-4400. Breakfast/Lunch. $

Listed Alphabetically (cont.)

Penny's Noodle Shop, 22.
3400 N Sheffield Ave
☎ 773/281-8222. Pan-Asian. $

Piazza Bella, 34. 2116 W Roscoe St
☎ 773/477-7330. Italian. $-$$

Riccardo Trattoria, 44. 2119 N Clark
St ☎ 773/549-0038. Italian. $$-$$$

Sai Café, 41. 2010 N Sheffield Ave
☎ 773/472-8080. Japanese. $$-$$$

Salt & Papper Diner, 33.
2575 N Lincoln Ave ☎ 773/525-8788.
American. $

Tallulah, 14. 4539 N Lincoln Ave
☎ 773/942-7585. American. $$$$

Thai Classic, 23. 3332 N Clark St
☎ 773/404-2000. Thai. $

Tomboy, 7. 5402 N Clark St
☎ 773/907-0636. American. $$-$$$

Tre Kronor, 5. 3258 W Foster Ave
☎ 773/267-9888. Scandinavian. $

Udupi Palace, 4. 2543 W Devon Ave
☎ 773/338-2152. Indian/Vegetarian. $

Viceroy of India, 3.
2516 W Devon Ave ☎ 773/743-4100.
Indian. $

Vinci, 51. 1732 N Halsted St
☎ 266-1199. Italian. $-$$

Wishbone, 24. 33 N Lincoln Ave
☎ 773/549-4105. Southern. $

Yoshi's Café, 26. 3257 N Halsted St
Eclectic. $$

BUCKTOWN & WICKER PARK

Adobo Grill Wicker Park, 76.
2005 W Division St ☎ 773/252-9990.
Mexican/Tex Mex. $-$$

Blue Fin, 70. 1952 W North Ave
☎ 773/394-7373. Sushi. $-$$

Bob San, 79. 1805 W Division St
☎ 773/235-8888. Sushi. $$-$$$

Bongo Room, 67.
1470 N Milwaukee Ave
☎ 773/489-0690. Breakfast/Lunch. $

Cafe Absinthe, 71. 1954 W North Ave
☎ 773/278-4488. French. $$-$$$

Cafe Matou, 61.
1846 N Milwaukee Ave
☎ 773/384-8911. French. $$-$$$

Club Lucky, 63.
1824 W Wabansia Ave
☎ 773/227-2300. Italian. $$-$$$

Coast, 57. 2045 N Damen Ave
☎ 773/235-5775. Sushi. $$-$$$

Feast, 72. 1616 N Damen Ave
☎ 773/772-7100. Eclectic. $-$$

Francesca's Forno, 73.
1576 N Milwaukee Ave
☎ 773/770-0184. Italian. $$-$$$

Handlebar, 77. 2311 W North Ave
☎ 773/384-9546. Vegetarian. $

Jane's, 56. 1655 W Cortland Ave
☎ 773/862-JANE. American. $$

La Brochette, 80.
1401 N Ashland Ave ☎ 773/276-5650.
Mediterranean. $-$$

Le Bouchon, 59. 1958 N Damen Ave
☎ 773/862-6600. Bistro. $

Mado, 69. 1647 N Milwaukee Ave
☎ 773/342-2340. Eclectic. $-$$

Mirai, 75. 2020 W Division St
☎ 773/862-8500. Japanese. $$

Parlor, 66. 1745 W North Ave
☎ 773/782-9000. American. $$-$$$

Rinconcito Sudamericano, 58.
1954 W Armitage Ave
☎ 773/489-3126. Peruvian. $

Rodan, 68. 1530 N Milwaukee Ave
☎ 773/276-7036. Pan Asian. $-$$

Schwa, 65.
1466 N Ashland Ave ☎ 773/252-1466.
American Contemporary. $$$$

Silver Cloud, 62. 1700 N Damen Ave
☎ 773/489-6212. American.$-$$

Smoke Daddy, 79. 1804 W Division St
Barbecue. $-$$

Spring, 74. 2039 W North Ave
☎ 773/395-7100.
Contemporary.$$$-$$$$

Takashi Restaurant, 60. 1952 N
Damen Ave ☎ 773/772-6170.
American Contemporary. $$-$$$

Zen Noodles, 64. 1852 W North Ave
☎ 773/276-8300. Pan-Asian. $

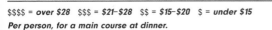

$$$$ = over $28 $$$ = $21-$28 $$ = $15-$20 $ = under $15
Per person, for a main course at dinner.

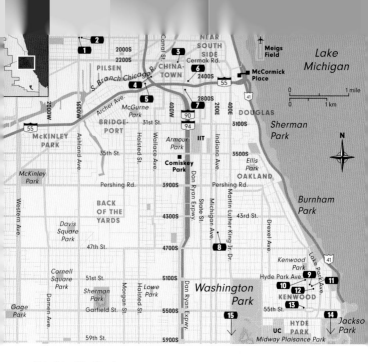

Listed by Site Number

1. Nuevo Leon
2. Playa Azul
3. Happy Chef Dim Sum
4. Phoenix
5. Lao Sze Chuan
6. Emperor's Choice
7. House of Fortune
8. Gladys Luncheonette
9. Park 52
10. Original Pancake House
11. Calypso Cafe
12. Dixie Kitchen & Bait Shop
13. La Petite Folie
14. Soul Queen
15. Army & Lou's

Listed Alphabetically

Army & Lou's, 15. 420 E 75th St
☎ 773/483-3100. Soul Food. $-$$

Calypso Cafe, 11.
5211 S Harper Ave ☎ 773/955-0229.
Cajun. $-$$

Dixie Kitchen & Bait Shop, 12.
5225 S Harper Ave ☎ 773/363-4943.
Caribbean. $-$$

Emperor's Choice, 6.
2238 S Wentworth Ave ☎ 225-8800.
Chinese. $-$$

Gladys Luncheonette, 8.
4527 S Indiana Ave ☎ 773/548-4566.
Soul Food. $

Happy Chef Dim Sum, 3.
2164 S Archer Ave. ☎ 808-3689.
Chinese. $

House of Fortune, 7.
2407 S Wentworth Ave. ☎ 225-0880.
Chinese. $-$$$

La Petite Folie, 13. 1504 E 55 St
☎ 773/493-1394. French. $$-$$$

Lao Sze Chuan, 5.
2172 S Archer Ave ☎ 326-5040.
Chinese. $

Nuevo Leon, 1.
1515 W 18th St ☎ 421-1517.
Mexican. $

Original Pancake House, 10.
1517 E Hyde Park Blvd
☎ 773/288-2323. Breakfast. $

Park 52, 9. 5201 S Harper Ct
☎ 773/241-5200.
Classic American. $$$

Phoenix, 4. 2131 S Archer Ave
☎ 328-0848. Chinese. $-$$

Playa Azul, 2. 1514 W 18th St
☎ 421-2552. Mexican. $

Soul Queen, 14. 9031 S Stony Island
Ave ☎ 773/731-3366. Soul Food. $-$$

$$$$ = over $28 $$$ = $21-$28 $$ = $15-$20 $ = under $15

Per person, for a main course at dinner.

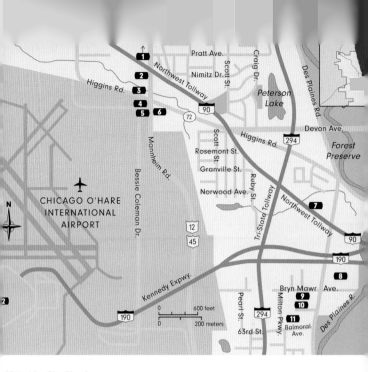

Listed by Site Number

1 Radisson Hotel Chicago O'Hare

2 Wyndham O'Hare Rosemount

3 Best Western at O'Hare

4 Holiday Inn Express

5 O'Hare Marriott

6 Sheraton Gateway Suites

7 Westin O'Hare Hotel

8 Hyatt Regency O'Hare

9 Sofitel Chicago O'Hare

10 Embassy O'Hare

11 Crowne Plaza Chicago O'Hare

12 Hilton Chicago O'Hare Airport

Listed Alphabetically

Best Western at O'Hare, 3.
10300 W Higgins Rd, Rosemont
☎ 847/296-4471. 🖷 847/296-4958. $$

Crowne Plaza Chicago O'Hare, 11.
5440 N River Rd, Rosemont
☎ 847/671-6350. 🖷 847/671-5406.
$$-$$$

Embassy O'Hare, 10. 5500 N River
Rd, Rosemont ☎ 847/678-4000.
🖷 847/928-7659. $$-$$$

Hilton Chicago O'Hare Airport, 12.
O'Hare Int'l Airport ☎ 773/601-2873.
🖷 773/601-2873. $$-$$$

Holiday Inn Express, 4.
6600 N Mannheim Rd, Rosemont
☎ 847/544-7500. 🖷 847/544-7544. $$

Hyatt Regency O'Hare, 8.
9300 W Bryn Mawr Ave, Rosemont
☎ 847/696-1234. 🖷 847/696-0139.
$$-$$$

O'Hare Marriott, 5.
8535 W Higgins Rd ☎ 773/693-4444.
🖷 847/693-3164. $$-$$$

Radisson Hotel Chicago O'Hare, 1.
1450 E Touhy Ave, Des Plaines
☎ 847/296-8866. 🖷 847/296-8268.
$-$$

Sheraton Gateway Suites, 6.
6501 N Mannheim Rd, Rosemont
☎ 847/699-6300. 🖷 847/699-0391.
$$-$$$$

Sofitel Chicago O'Hare, 9.
5550 N River Rd, Rosemont
☎ 847/678-4488. 🖷 847/678-4244. $$$

Westin O'Hare Hotel, 7.
6100 N River Rd, Rosemont
☎ 847/698-6000. 🖷 847/698-3993.
$$-$$$$

Wyndham O'Hare Rosemount, 2.
6810 N Mannheim Rd, Rosemont
☎ 847/297-1234. 🖷 847/297-1234. $$$

$$$$ = *over $260* $$$ = *$180–$260* $$ = *$100–$179* $ = *under $100*
All prices are for a standard double room, excluding 14.9% room tax.

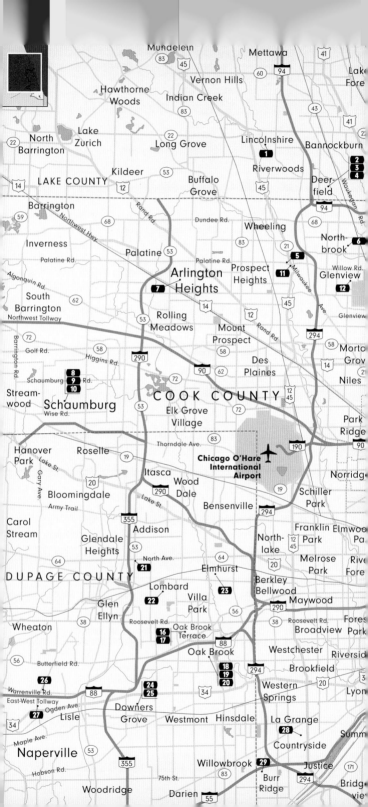

Lake Michigan

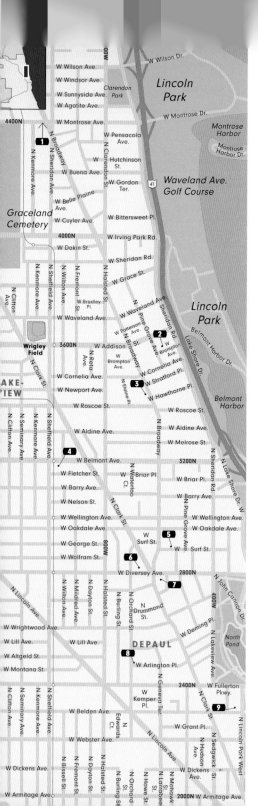

Listed by Site Number

NORTH SIDE

1 Chicago International Hostel
2 The Majestic
3 Best Western-Hawthorne Terrace
4 City Suites Hotel
5 The Willows
6 Days Inn Lincoln Park North
7 Inn at Lincoln Park
8 Arlington House
9 Belden-Stratford

DOWNTOWN & NEAR NORTH

10 Ambassador East
11 Hotel Indigo
12 Sutton Place Hotel
13 The Drake
14 Westin Michigan Avenue
15 Millenium Knickerbocker Hotel
16 Raffaello Condo Hotel
17 Hilton Suites Chicago
18 Four Seasons
19 Talbott
20 Whitehall Hotel
21 Sofitel Chicago Water Tower
22 Tremont
23 Ritz-Carlton
24 Seneca
25 Park Hyatt Chicago
26 The Peninsula Chicago
27 HoJo Inn
28 Allerton Crowne Plaza
29 Affinia Chicago
30 Omni Chicago Hotel
31 Holiday Inn Express-Cass Hotel
32 Embassy Suites
33 Best Western River North Hotel
34 Hilton Garden Inn
35 Homewood Suites by Hilton
36 The James

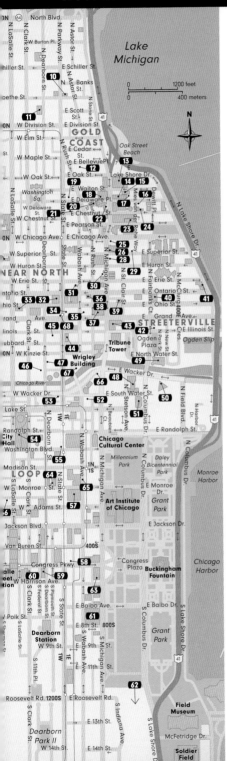

**Listed by
Site Number
(cont.)**

37 Chicago
Marriott
Downtown

38 Conrad

39 Best Western Inn
of Chicago

40 Doubletree Hotel

41 W Chicago Lake
Shore

42 Embassy Suites
Lakefront

43 Hotel
Inter-Continental
Chicago

44 Courtyard by
Marriott Chicago
Downtown

45 Hampton Inn
& Suites

46 Westin River North

47 Hotel Sax Chicago

48 Hyatt Regency

49 Sheraton Chicago
Hotel and
Towers

50 Swissôtel

51 Fairmont

52 Hotel Monaco

53 Renaissance
Chicago Hotel

54 Hotel Allegro
Chicago

55 Hotel Burnham

56 W Chicago
City Center

57 Palmer House Hilton

58 Hostelling
International–
Chicago

59 Hotel Blake

60 Holiday Inn & Suites
Downtown Chicago

61 Chicago Hilton
and Towers

62 Hyatt Regency
McCormick Place

63 Blackstone Hotel

64 Hampton Majestic

65 Silversmith

66 Hotel 71

67 Trump Hotel

68 Dana Hotel

Listed Alphabetically

GREATER CHICAGO

Carelton of Oak Park, 30.
1110 Pleasant St, Oak Park
☎ 708/848-5000. 🖷 708/848-0537.
$-$$$

Comfort Suites Lombard, 21.
530 W North Ave, Lombard
☎ 630/268-1300. 🖷 630/268-1400.
$-$$$

Countryside Holiday Inn, 28.
6201 Joliet Rd, Countryside
☎ 708/354-4200. 🖷 708/354-4241. $$

Courtyard Elmhurst, 23.
IL Rte 83 at North Ave, Elmhurst
☎ 630/941-9444. 🖷 630/941-3539.
$-$$$

Doubletree-Downers Grove, 24.
2111 Butterfield Rd, Downers Grove
☎ 630/971-2000. 🖷 630/971-1168. $$

Doubletree-Oak Brook, 19.
1909 Spring Rd, Oak Brook
☎ 630/472-6000. 🖷 630/573-1133.
$$-$$$

Doubletree-Schaumburg, 10.
800 National Pkwy, Schaumburg
☎ 847/605-9222. 🖷 847/605-9240.
$-$$

Embassy Suites, 4.
1445 Lake Cook Rd, Deerfield
☎ 847/945-4500. 🖷 847/945-8189.
$-$$

Embassy Suites, 22.
707 E Butterfield Rd, Lombard
☎ 630/969-7500. 🖷 630/969-8776. $$

Hilton Lisle Naperville, 26.
3003 Corporate West Drive, Lisle
☎ 630/505-0900. 🖷 630/505-8948.
$$-$$$$

Hilton Suites, 16. 10 Drury Lane,
Oakbrook Terrace ☎ 630/941-0100.
🖷 630/941-0299. $$-$$$

Holiday Inn, 17. 17 W 350 22nd St,
Oakbrook Terrace ☎ 630/ 833-3600.
🖷 630/833-7037. $$

Holiday Inn North Shores, 15.
5300 W. Touhy Ave, Skokie
☎ 847/ 679-8900.
🖷 847/679-7447. $-$$$

Holiday Inn Select Naperville, 27.
1801 Naper Blvd, Naperville
☎ 630/ 505-4900. 🖷 630/505-8239.
$$-$$$

Hyatt, 3.
1750 Lake Cook Rd, Deerfield
☎ 847/945-3400. 🖷 847/945-3563.
$$-$$$

Hyatt Regency Woodfield, 9.
1800 E Golf Rd, Schaumburg
☎ 847/605-1234. 🖷 847/605-0328.
$$-$$$$

Jameson Inn, 7.
2111 Arlington Heights Rd, Arlington
Heights ☎ 847/956-1400.
🖷 847/956-0804. $

Marriott-Schaumburg Suites, 8.
50 N Martingale Rd, Schaumburg
☎ 847/240-0100. 🖷 847/240-2388.
$-$$

Marriott Suites, 2.
2 Parkway N, Deerfield
☎ 847/405-9666. 🖷 847/405-0354.
$-$$

Marriott Suites, 25.
1500 Opus Place, Downers Grove
☎ 630/852-1500. 🖷 630/852-6527 $$

Marriott's Lincolnshire Resort, 1.
10 Marriott Dr, Lincolnshire
☎ 847/ 634-0100. 🖷 847/634-1278. $$

North Shore Doubletree, 13.
9599 Skokie Blvd, Skokie
☎ 847/679-7000. 🖷 847/679-9841. $$

Northbrook Hilton, 5.
2855 N Milwaukee Ave, Northbrook
☎ 847/480-7500. 🖷 847/480-0827. $$

Oak Brook Hills Marriott Resort, 20.
3500 Midwest Rd, Oak Brook
☎ 630/850-5555. 🖷 630/850-5569.
$$$

**The Oaks Hotel & Conference Ctr,
29.** 300 S Frontage Rd, Burr Ridge
☎ 630/325-2900. 🖷 630/325-8907.
$$-$$$

Omni Orrington, 14.
1710 Orrington Ave, Evanston
☎ 847/866-8700. 🖷 847/866-8724. $$

Radisson Hotel Northbrook, 11.
2875 N Milwaukee Ave, Northbrook
☎ 847/298-2525. 🖷 847/298-8965.
$$-$$$

Renaissance North Shore Chicago, 6.
933 Skokie Rd, Northbrook
☎ 847/498-6500. 🖷 847/498-9558. $$

Renaissance Oak Brook, 18.
2100 Spring Rd, Oak Brook
☎ 630/573-2800. 🖷 630/573-7134.
$-$$$

Wyndham Glenview Suites, 12.
1400 Milwaukee Ave, Glenview
☎ 847/803-9800. 🖷 847/803-0380.
$$-$$$

Listed Alphabetically (cont.)

NORTH SIDE, DOWNTOWN & NEAR NORTH

Affinia Chicago, 29.
166 E Superior St ☎ 787–6000.
📠787–6133. $$$$

Allerton Crowne Plaza, 28.
701 N Michigan Ave ☎ 440–1500.
📠440–1819. $$–$$$$

Ambassador East, 10.
1301 N State Pkwy ☎ 787–7200.
📠787–4760. $$$$

Arlington House Hostel, 8.
66 W Arlington Place
☎ 773/929–5380. 📠773/665–5485. $

Belden-Stratford, 9.
2300 N Lincoln Park W
☎ 773/281–2900. 📠773/880–2039. $$

Best Western Hawthorne Terrace, 3.
3434 N Braodway ☎ 888/860–3400.
📠773/244–3435. $$$

Best Western Inn of Chicago, 39.
162 E Ohio St ☎ 787–3100.
📠573–3136. $$–$$$

Best Western River North, 33.
125 W Ohio St ☎ 467–0800.
📠467–1665. $$–$$$$

Blackstone Hotel, 63.
636 S Michigan Ave ☎ 447–0955.
📠765–0545. $$–$$$$

Chicago Hilton and Towers, 61.
720 S Michigan Ave ☎ 922–4400.
📠922–5240. $$$–$$$$

Chicago International Hostel, 1.
6318 N Winthrop Ave ☎ 773/262–1011.
📠773/262–3673. $

Chicago Marriott Downtown, 37.
540 N Michigan Ave ☎ 836–0100.
📠836–6139. $$$$

City Suites Hotel, 4.
933 W Belmont Ave ☎ 773/404–3400.
📠773/404–3405. $$–$$$

Conrad, 38. 521 N Rush St
☎ 645–1500. 📠345–1550. $$$–$$$$

Courtyard by Marriott Chicago Downtown, 44. 30 E Hubbard St
☎ 329–2500. 📠329–0293. $$–$$$$

Dana Hotel, 68. 660 N State St
☎ 202–6004, 888/286–2589.
📠202–6033. $$$$

Days Inn Lincoln Park North, 6.
644 W Diversey Pkwy
☎ 773/525–7010. 📠773/525–6998. $$

Doubletree Hotel, 40.
300 E Ohio St ☎ 787–6100.
📠787–6238. $$–$$$

The Drake, 13. 140 E Walton Pl
☎ 787–2200. 📠787–1431. $$$$

Embassy Suites, 32. 600 N State St
☎ 943–3800. 📠943–7629. $$$–$$$$

Embassy Suites Lakefront, 42.
511 N Columbus Dr ☎ 836–5900.
📠836–5901. $$–$$$

Fairmont, 51. 200 N Columbus Dr
☎ 565–8000. 📠856–1032. $$$–$$$$

Four Seasons, 18.
120 E Delaware Pl
☎ 280–8800. 📠280–1748. $$$$

Hampton Inn and Suites, 45.
33 W Illinois St ☎ 832–0330.
📠832–0333. $$

Hampton Majestic, 64.
22 W Monroe St ☎ 332–5052.
📠332–5051. $$–$$$

Hilton Garden Inn, 34.
10 E Grand Ave ☎ 595–0000.
📠595–0955. $$–$$$

Hilton Suites Chicago, 17.
198 E Delaware ☎ 664–1100.
📠664–9881. $$$–$$$$

HoJo Inn, 27. 720 N LaSalle St
☎ 664–8100. 📠664–2356. $$–$$$

Holiday Inn and Suites Downtown Chicago, 60. 506 W Harrison St
☎ 957–9100. 📠957–0474. $$–$$$

Holiday Inn Express-Cass Hotel, 31.
640 N Wabash Ave ☎ 787–4030.
📠787–8544. $$$

Homewood Suites by Hilton, 35.
40 E Grand Ave ☎ 644–2222.
📠664–7777. $$$–$$$$

Hostelling International Chicago, 58.
24 E Congress Pkwy ☎ 360–0300.
📠360–0313. $

Hotel Allegro Chicago, 54.
171 W Randolph St ☎ 236–0123.
📠236–0197. $$$–$$$$

Hotel Blake, 59. 500 S Dearborn St
☎ 986–1234. 📠939–2468. $$$$

Hotel Burnham, 55.
1 W Washington Blvd ☎ 782–1111.
📠782–0899. $$$–$$$$

Hotel Indigo, 11. 1244 N Dearborn
Pkwy ☎ 787–4980. 📠787–4069. $$$

$$$$ = *over $260* $$$ = *$180–$260* $$ = *$100–$179* $ = *under $100*
All prices are for a standard double room, excluding 15.4% room tax.

Listed Alphabetically

Hotel Inter-Continental Chicago, 43. 505 N Michigan Ave ☎ 866/210-8811. ☏944-1320. $$$$

Hotel Monaco, 52. 225 N Wabash Ave ☎ 960-8500. ☏960-1883. $$$$

Hotel Sax Chicago, 47. 333 N Dearborn St ☎ 245-0333. ☏923-2444. $$$-$$$$

Hotel 71, 66. 71 E Wacker Dr ☎ 346-7100. ☏346-1721. $$-$$$$

Hyatt Regency, 48. 151 E Wacker Dr ☎ 565-1234. ☏239-4414. $$$$

Hyatt Regency McCormick Place, 62. 2233 S King Dr ☎ 567-1234. ☏528-4000. $$-$$$$

Inn at Lincoln Park, 7. 601 W Diversey Pkwy ☎ 866/774-PARK. ☏773/348-1912. $-$$

The James, 36. 55 E Ontario St ☎ 337-1000. ☏337-7217. $$$-$$$$

The Majestic, 2. 528 W Brompton Ave ☎ 773/404-3499. ☏773/404-3495. $$-$$$

Millennium Knickerbocker Hotel, 15. 163 E Walton Pl ☎ 751-8100. ☏751-9205. $$$-$$$$

Omni Chicago Hotel, 30. 676 N Michigan Ave ☎ 944-6664. ☏266-3015. $$$-$$$$

Palmer House Hilton, 57. 17 E Monroe St ☎ 726-7500. ☏917-1707. $$$$

Park Hyatt Chicago, 25. 800 N Michigan Ave ☎ 335-1234. ☏239-4000. $$$$

The Peninsula Chicago, 26. 108 E Superior St ☎ 337-2888. ☏751-2888. $$$$

Raffaello Condo Hotel, 16. 201 E Delaware Pl ☎ 943-5000. ☏943-9483. $$$

Renaissance Chicago Hotel, 53. 1 W Wacker Dr ☎ 372-7200. ☏372-0093. $$$-$$$$

Ritz-Carlton, 23. 160 E Pearson St ☎ 266-1000. ☏266-1194. $$$$

Seneca, 24. 200 E Chestnut St ☎ 787-8900. ☏988-4438. $$-$$$$

Sheraton Chicago Hotel and Towers, 49. 301 E North Water St ☎ 464-1000. ☏464-9140. $$$$

Silversmith Hotel, 65. 10 S S Wabash Ave ☎ 795-6500. ☏372-7320. $$-$$$

Sofitel Chicago Water Tower, 21. 20 E Chestnut St ☎ 324-4000. ☏324-4026. $$$$

Sutton Place Hotel, 12. 21 E Bellevue Pl ☎ 266-2100. ☏266-2103. $$$$

Swissôtel, 50. 323 E Wacker Dr ☎ 565-0565. ☏565-0540. $$$$

Talbott, 19. 20 E Delaware Pl ☎ 944-4970. ☏944-7241. $$$$

Tremont, 22. 100 E Chestnut St ☎ 751-1900. ☏751-8691. $$-$$$

Trump Hotel, 67. 401 N Wabash Ave ☎ 588-8000. ☏588-8001. $$$$

W Chicago City Center, 56. 172 W Adams St ☎ 332-1200. ☏917-5771. $$$$

W Chicago Lake Shore, 41. 644 N Lake Shore Drive ☎ 943-9200. ☏255-4411. $$$-$$$$

Westin Michigan Avenue, 14. 909 N Michigan Ave ☎ 943-7200. ☏397-5580. $$$$

Westin River North, 46. 320 N Dearborn St ☎ 744-1900. ☏527-2650. $$$$

Whitehall Hotel, 20. 105 E Delaware Pl ☎ 944-6300. ☏944-8552. $$$$

The Willows, 5. 555 W Surf St ☎ 773/528-8400. ☏773/528-8483. $$-$$$

$$$$ = *over $260* $$$ = *$180-$260* $$ = *$100-$179* $ = *under $100*
All prices are for a standard double room, excluding 15.4% room tax.

Listed by Site Number

1 Lifeline Theater
2 Raven Theatre
3 Ravinia Festival
4 Riviera Theatre
5 Neo-Futurarium
6 Aragon Ballroom
7 Old Town School of Folk Music
8 Pegasus Players, O'Rourke Performing Arts Center
9 Black Ensemble Theater
10 Tinfish Theatre
11 Profiles Theatre
12 Strawdog Theatre Company
13 Live Bait Theater
14 American Theater Company
15 Mercury Theater
16 Stage Left Theatre
17 Briar Street Theatre
18 The Playground Theater
19 Bailiwick Repertory
20 Theatre Building
21 The Vic
22 Athenaeum Theatre
23 Timeline Theatre Company
24 Theater on the Lake
25 Apollo Theater
26 Victory Gardens Biograph Theater
27 Park West
28 Victory Gardens Greenhouse Theater
29 Royal George Theatre
30 Steppenwolf Theatre Company
31 Lookingglass Theater Company
32 Chicago Center For the Performing Arts
33 Chicago Dramatists Theatre
34 Chicago Shakespeare Theater
53 Court Theatre
54 ETA Creative Arts Foundation
55 Redmoon Theater
56 Chopin Theatre
57 Prop Thtr

MAP **54** **Performing Arts/Downtown**

Listed by Site Number

35 Civic Opera House

36 Cadillac Palace Theatre

37 Goodman Theatre

38 Ford Center— Oriental Theatre

39 Storefront Theatre

40 Chicago Theatre

41 Chicago Cultural Center

42 Silk Road Theater Project

43 Bank of America (Schubert) Theatre

44 Harris Theater for Music and Dance

45 Auditorium Theatre

46 DePaul University Merle Reskin Theatre

47 Symphony Center

48 Getz Theater at Columbia College

49 Dance Center of Columbia College

50 Arie Crown Theater

51 UIC Theater

52 Building Stage

Listed Alphabetically

American Theater Company, 14.
1909 W Byron St ☎ 773/929-1031

Apollo Theater, 25.
2540 N Lincoln Ave ☎ 773/935-6100

Aragon Ballroom, 6.
1106 W Lawrence Ave ☎ 773/561-9500

Arie Crown Theater, 50.
McCormick Place, 2301 S Lake Shore Dr
☎ 791-6190

Athenaeum Theatre, 22.
2936 N Southport Ave
☎ 773/935-6860

Auditorium Theatre, 45.
50 E Congress Pkwy ☎ 902-1500

Bailiwick Repertory, 19.
1229 W Belmont Ave ☎ 773/883-1090

**Bank of America
(Schubert) Theatre, 43.**
22 W Monroe St ☎ 902-1400

Black Ensemble Theater, 9.
4520 N Beacon St ☎ 773/769-4451

Briar Street Theatre, 17
3133 N Halsted St ☎ 773/348-4000

Listed Alphabetically (cont.)

Building Stage, 52.
412 N Carpenter St ☎ 491–1369

Cadillac Palace Theatre, 36.
151 W Randolph St ☎ 902–1400

Chicago Cultural Center, 41.
78 E Washington Blvd ☎ 346–3278

Chicago Dramatists, 33.
1105 W Chicago Ave ☎ 663–0630

**Chicago Center for the
Performing Arts, 32.**
777 N Green ☎ 733–6000

Chicago Shakespeare Theater, 34.
800 E Grand Ave ☎ 595–5600

Chicago Theatre, 40.
175 N State St ☎ 462–6300

Chopin Theatre, 56.
1543 W Division St ☎ 773/278–1500

Civic Opera House/Lyric Opera, 35.
20 N Wacker Dr ☎ 332–2244 x5600

Court Theatre, 53.
5535 S Ellis Ave ☎ 773/753–4472

**Dance Center of
Columbia College, 49.**
1306 S Michigan Ave ☎ 344–8300

**De Paul University
Merle Reskin Theater, 46.**
60 E Balbo Ave ☎ 922–1999

ETA Creative Arts Foundation, 54.
7558 S South Chicago Ave
☎ 773/752–3955

Ford Center-Oriental Theatre, 38.
24 W Randolph St ☎ 902–1400

Getz Theater at Columbia College, 48. 72 E 11th St ☎ 663–1600, ext. 6126

Goodman Theatre, 37.
170 N Dearborn St ☎ 443–3800

**Harris Theater for Music
and Dance, 44.**
205 E Randolph St ☎ 334–7777

Lifeline Theater, 1.
6912 N Glenwood Ave ☎ 773/761–4477

Live Bait Theater, 13.
3914 N Clark St ☎ 773/871–1212

Lookingglass Theater Company, 31.
821 N Michigan Ave ☎ 337–0665

Mercury Theater, 15.
3745 N Southport Ave ☎ 773/325–1700

Neo-Futurarium, 5.
5153 N Ashland Ave ☎ 773/275–5255

Old Town School of Folk Music, 7.
4544 N Lincoln Ave ☎ 773/728–6000

Park West, 27.
322 W Armitage Ave ☎ 773/929–5959

**Pegasus Players, O'Rourke
Performing Arts Center, 8.**
1145 W Wilson Ave
☎ 773/878–9761

The Playground Improv Theater, 18.
3209 N Halsted St ☎ 773/871–3793

Profiles Theatre, 11.
4147 N Broadway ☎ 773/549–1815

Prop Thtr, 57. 3504 N Elston Ave
☎ 773/539–7838

Raven Theatre, 2.
6157 N Clark St ☎ 773/338–2177

Ravinia Festival, 3.
Lake-Cook & Green Bay Rds,
Highland Park ☎ 847/266–5100

Redmoon Theater, 55.
1463 W Hubbard Ave ☎ 850–8440

Riviera Theatre, 4.
4746 N Racine Ave ☎ 773/275–8600

Royal George Theatre, 29.
1641 N Halsted St ☎ 988–9000

Silk Road Theatre Project, 42.
77 W Washington Blvd. ☎ 857–1234

Stage Left Theatre, 16.
3408 N Sheffield Ave
☎ 773/883–8830

Steppenwolf Theatre Company, 30.
1650 N Halsted St ☎ 335–1650

Storefront Theater, 39.
66 E Randolph St ☎ 742–8497

Strawdog Theatre Company, 12.
3829 N Broadway ☎ 773/528–9696

Symphony Center, 47.
220 S Michigan Ave ☎ 294–3000

Theater on the Lake, 24.
Fullerton Ave and Lake Shore Dr
☎ 742–7994

Theatre Building, 20.
1225 W Belmont Ave ☎ 773/327–5252

Timeline Theatre Company, 23.
615 W Wellington Ave ☎ 773/281–8463

Tinfish Theatre, 10.
4247 N Lincoln Ave ☎ 773/549–1888

UIC Theater, 51.
1044 W Harrison St ☎ 996–2939

The Vic, 21.
3145 N Sheffield Ave ☎ 773/472–0449.

**Victory Gardens
Biograph Theater, 26.**
2433 N Lincoln Ave ☎ 773/871–3000

**Victory Gardens Greenhouse
Theater, 28.** 2257 N Lincoln Ave
☎ 773/871–3000

Listed by Site Number

1 Village North
2 Lincoln Village
3 Gateway/Copernicus Center
4 Davis
5 Music Box
6 Vic Theatre
7 City North 14
8 Landmark's Century Centre
9 Bank of America Cinema
10 Logan
11 Facets Cinematheque
12 Showplace 14 Galewood Crossing
13 Ford City
14 Webster Place
15 Pipers Alley
16 Beverly Arts Center
17 Chatham 14
18 Muvico Theaters
19 Alliance Francaise
20 600 N Michigan Ave
21 River East 21
22 Navy Pier Imax
23 Instituto Italiano di Cultura
24 Chicago Cultural Ctr
25 Gene Siskel Film Center at the School of the Art Institute
26 Harold Washington Library Center
27 Kerasotes ShowPlace Theaters at Roosevelt Collection
28 Henry Crown Omnimax
29 University of Chicago Doc Films

Listed Alphabetically

Alliance Francaise, 19.
54 W Chicago Ave ☎ 337–1070

Bank of America Cinema, 9.
4901 W Irving Park Rd ☎ 904–9442

Beverly Arts Center, 16.
2407 W 111th St ☎ 773/445–3838

Chatham 14, 17.
210 W 87th St ☎ 773/783–8711

Chicago Cultural Center, 24.
78 E Washington Blvd ☎ 744–6630

City North 14, 7.
2600 N Western Ave
☎ 800/326–3264 x1642

Davis, 4. 4614 N Lincoln Ave
☎ 773/784–0893

Facets Cinematheque, 11.
1517 W Fullerton Ave ☎ 773/281–4114

Ford City, 13.
7601 S Cicero Ave ☎ 773/582–1839

Gateway/Copernicus Center, 3.
5216 W Lawrence Ave ☎ 773/777–9438

Gene Siskel Film Center at the School of the Art Institute, 25.
164 N State St ☎ 846–2800

Harold Washington Library Center, 26.
400 S State St ☎ 747–4100

Henry Crown Omnimax Museum of Science and Industry, 28.
5700 S Lakeshore Dr ☎ 773/684–1414

Instituto Italiano di Cultura, 23.
500 N Michigan Ave ☎ 822–9545

Kerasotes ShowPlace Theaters at Roosevelt Collection, 27.
1011 S Delano Court E (open fall 2009)

Landmark's Century Centre, 8.
2828 N Clark St ☎ 773/509–4949

Lincoln Village, 2.
6341 N McCormick St ☎ 773/604–4741

Logan, 10.
2646 N Milwaukee Ave
☎ 773/252–0627

Music Box, 5.
3733 N Southport Ave
☎ 773/871–6604

Muvico Theaters, 18.
108 N State St (open spring 2009)

Navy Pier Imax, 22.
700 E Grand Ave ☎ 595–5629

Pipers Alley, 15.
1608 Wells St ☎ 642–7500

River East 21, 21.
322 E Illinois St ☎ 596–0333

ShowPlace 14 Galewood Crossing, 12. 5530 W Homer St
☎ 800/326–3264 x1646

600 North Michigan Avenue, 20.
600 N Michigan Ave ☎ 255–9340

University of Chicago Doc Films, 29.
1212 E 59th St ☎ 773/702–8575

Vic Theatre, 6.
3145 N Sheffield Ave ☎ 773/929–6713

Village North, 1.
6746 N Sheridan Rd ☎ 773/764–9100

Webster Place, 14.
1471 W Webster Ave
☎ 800/326–3264 x1641

MAP 56 Nightlife/Near North & Downtown

MAP 56

Listed by Site Number

1 Pump Room
2 Third Coast Café
3 Underground Wonder Bar
4 Coq d'Or at the Drake
5 Le Passage
6 Evil Olive
7 Blue Chicago
8 Enclave
9 Excalibur
10 Spy Bar
11 Sand-Bar
12 Blue Chicago on Clark
13 Jazz Showcase
14 Pops for Champagne
15 Baton Show Lounge
16 House of Blues
17 The Underground
18 Andy's
19 Gentry
20 La Pomme Rouge
21 ESPN Zone
22 Rockit Bar
23 Joe's Be-Bop Cafe & Jazz Emporium
24 Funky Buddha Lounge
25 Transit
26 The Tasting Room
27 Wet Nightclub
28 Encore
29 Buddy Guy's Legends
30 Reggies Music Joint
31 Velvet Lounge

Listed Alphabetically

Andy's, 18.
11 E Hubbard St ☎ 642-6805. Jazz

Baton Show Lounge, 15.
436 N Clark St ☎ 644-5269.
Drag Club

Blue Chicago, 7.
736 N Clark St ☎ 642-6261. Blues

Blue Chicago on Clark, 12.
534 N Clark St ☎ 661-1003. Blues

Buddy Guy's Legends, 29.
754 S Wabash Ave ☎ 427-0333. Blues

Coq d'Or at the Drake, 4.
140 E Walton St ☎ 932-4623
Piano Bar

Enclave, 8.
222 W Chicago Ave
☎ 654-0234. Dance Club

Encore, 28.
171 W Randolph St
☎ 338-3788. Lounge

ESPN Zone, 21. 43 E Ohio St
☎ 644-ESPN. Sports Bar

Evil Olive, 6. 1551 W Division St
☎ 773/235-9100. DJ

Excalibur, 9. 632 N Dearborn St
☎ 266-1944. Dance Club

Funky Buddha Lounge, 24.
728 W Grand Ave ☎ 666-1695.
Dance Club

Gentry, 19.
440 N State St ☎ 836-0993.
Gay/Piano Bar/Cabaret

House of Blues, 16.
329 N Dearborn St
☎ 923-2000. Blues/Roots Music

Jazz Showcase, 13.
806 S Plymouth Ct ☎ 360-0234. Jazz

Joe's Be-Bop Cafe & Jazz Emporium, 23.
600 E Grand Ave
☎ 595-5299. Jazz

La Pomme Rouge, 20. 108 W Kinzie
St ☎ 245-9555. Dessert Bar/Lounge

Le Passage, 5. 937 N Rush St
☎ 255-0022. DJ/Dance Club

Pops for Champagne, 14.
601 N State St ☎ 266-7677. Jazz

Pump Room, 1. 1301 N State Pkwy
☎ 266-0360. Piano Bar/Jazz

Reggies Music Joint, 30.
2105 S State St ☎ 949-0120.
Indie Rock/Blues/Punk

Rockit Bar & Grill, 22.
22 W Hubbard St ☎ 645-6000. DJ

Sand-Bar, 11. 226 W Ontario St
☎ 787-4480. Dance Club

Spy Bar, 10. 646 N Franklin St
☎ 337-2191. Dance Club

The Tasting Room, 26.
1415 W Randolph St ☎ 942-1313
Wine Bar

Third Coast Café, 2.
1260 N Dearborn St ☎ 649-0730
Coffeehouse/Wine Bar

Transit, 25. 1431 W Lake St
☎ 491-8600. Dance Club

The Underground, 17.
56 W Illinois St ☎ 644-7600.
Bar/Lounge/Disco

Underground Wonder Bar, 3.
10 E Walton St ☎ 266-7761.
Live Music

Velvet Lounge, 31.
67 E Cermak Rd ☎ 791-9050.
Jazz/Blues

Wet Nightclub, 27. 209 W Lake St
☎ 223-9232. Dance Club

MAP **57** Nightlife/North Side

Kedzie Ave.

Virginia Ave.

West River Park

East River Park

41

Berwyn Ave.

Foster Ave.

Western Ave.

Damen Ave.
Winchester Ave.
Hoyne Ave.
Wolcott Ave.

Summerdale Ave.
Berwyn Ave.
41
5200W

Winnemac Park

Winnemac Ave.

ALBANY PARK

California Ave.

Ainslie St.
Rockwell St.

Oakley Ave.
Leavitt Ave.

Argyle St.
Ainslie St.

Hermitage Ave.
Paulina Ave.
Ravenswood Ave.

St. Boniface Cemetery

Clark St.

St. Louis Ave.
Kimball Ave.

Lawrence Ave.
Leland Ave.

Virginia Ave.
Manor Ave.

Lawrence Ave.

RAVENS- WOOD

4800W
5

Leland Ave.
Wilson Ave.
Sunnyside Ave.

Wilson Ave.

Welles Park

Sunnyside Ave.

Lincoln Ave.
1200W

Montrose Ave.
Cullom Ave.
Berteau Ave.
Belle Plaine Ave.

IRVING PARK

Spaulding Ave.
Kedzie Ave.
Albany Ave.
Sacramento Ave.
Francisco Ave.
California Ave.

2800W
Horner Park

Irving Park Rd.

3200W

Montrose Ave.
Cullom Ave.
Berteau Ave.
Belle Plaine Ave.

7 8

4000N

Cullom Ave.
Berteau Ave.
Belle Plaine Ave.

Byron St.

19

Byron St.

Paulina St.
Ravenswood Ave.

1600W

Byron St.
Grace St.

9

NORTH CENTER

Grace St.
Waveland Ave.

10

Waveland Ave.

Waveland Ave.

AVONDALE

Addison St.

Rockwell St.

Western Ave.

3600N

Cornelia Ave.
Oakley Ave.
Leavitt St.
Hoyne Ave.
Damen Ave.

Cornelia Ave.

Roscoe Ave.
School St.

Roscoe Ave.
School St.

29

Ravenswood Ave.
Paulina St.

Ashland Ave.

Greenview Ave.

27

3200N

28

31

Hamlin Park

Barry

Barry Ave.
Wellington Ave.

LOGAN SQUARE

Elston Ave.

Washtenaw Ave.
Rockwell St.

Wellington Ave.
George St.

Albany Ave.
Sacramento Ave.
Francisco Ave.

Wellington Ave.

George St.

Campbell Ave.

N. Branch Chicago R.

George St.

Wellington Ave.
George St.

2800N

Paulina St.

Greenview Ave.

St. Louis Ave.
Kedzie Ave.

Logan Sq.

Altgeld St.

John F. Kennedy Expwy.

2400N

43

41

44

Belden Ave.
Palmer St.
Dickens Ave.

45

Palmer Sq.

Humboldt Blvd.

42

47

Milwaukee Ave.

California Ave.

Belden Ave.

BUCKTOWN

Webster Ave.

Dickens Ave.

Leavitt St.
Hoyne Ave.
Damen Ave.

Armitage Ave.

Elston Ave.

90 94

64

Homan Ave.

Humboldt Park

Bloomingdale Ave.
Wabansia Ave.

Lemoyne St.
Hirsch St.
Potomac Ave.

Francisco Ave.

3200W

Sacramento Ave.

Armitage Ave.
Cortland St.
Bloomingdale Ave.
Wabansia Ave.

Campbell Ave.
Rockwell St.

2800W

LeMoyne
Hirsch St.
Potomac Ave.

North Ave.

Wabansia Ave.

48

Oakley Blvd.
Western Ave.

49

52

50
51

Wicker Park

Schiller St.
54

65

Cortland St.
Bloomingdale Ave.

46

Cortland St.
Bloomingdale Ave.

90 94

Lemoyne Ave.

53

UKRAINIAN VILLAGE

Ellen St.

Division St.

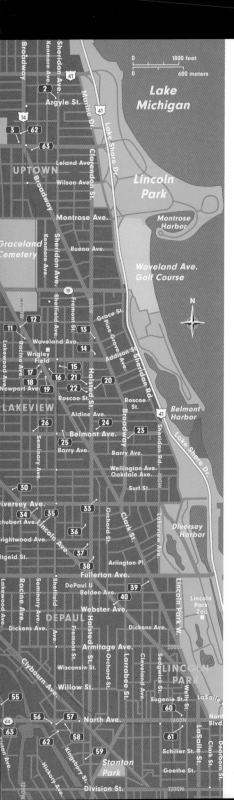

MAP 57

Listed by Site Number (cont.)

50 Double Door
51 Empire Liquors
52 The Flat Iron
53 Holiday Club
54 Davenport's
55 The Hideout
56 Joe's

57 Sangria Restaurant and Tapas Bar
58 Zentra
59 Boutique
60 Second City
61 Zanies
62 crobar

63 Exit
64 Prop House
65 Phyllis' Musical Inn

Listed Alphabetically

Abbey Pub, 6. 3420 W Grace St
☎ 773/478-4408. Irish/Celtic

Beat Kitchen, 29. 2100 W Belmont Ave
☎ 773/281-4444. Eclectic Live Music

Berlin, 26. 954 W Belmont Ave
☎ 773/348-4975. Dance Club

Big Chicks, 2. 5024 N Sheridan Rd
☎ 773/728-5511. Gay/Lesbian

BLUES, 38. 2519 N Halsted St
☎ 773/528-1012. Blues

The Bottom Lounge, 25.
1375 W Lake St ☎ 666-6775.
Live Music

Boutique, 59. 809 W Evergreen Ave
☎ 751-8700. DJ/Hip Hop

Carol's Pub, 5. 4659 N Clark St
☎ 773/334-2402. Country

Charlie's, 13. 3726 N Broadway
☎ 773/871-8887. Gay/DJ

Circuit, 14. 3641 N Halsted St
☎ 773/325-2233. Gay/DJ

The Closet, 23. 3325 N Broadway
☎ 773/477-8533. Gay

ComedySportz, 33. 929 Belmont St
☎ 773/549-8080. Improv Comedy

crobar, 62. 1543 N Kingsbury St
☎ 266-1900. Dance Club

Cubby Bear, 17. 1059 W Addison St
☎ 773/327-1662. Rock

Davenport's, 54.
1383 N Milwaukee Ave
☎ 773/278-1830. Cabaret/Piano Bar

Delilah's, 34. 2771 N Lincoln Ave
☎ 773/472-2771. DJ/Punk

Double Door, 50. 1572 N Milwaukee
Ave ☎ 773/489-3160. Rock

Elbo Room, 30. 2871 N Lincoln Ave
☎ 773/549-5549. Eclectic Live Music

Empire Liquors, 51.
1566 N Milwaukee Ave
☎ 773/278-1600. Lounge/DJ

Exedus II, 24. 3477 N Clark St
☎ 773/348-3998. Reggae

Exit, 63. 1315 W North Ave
☎ 773/395-2700. DJ/Punk

Fireside Bowl, 42.
2646 W Fullerton Ave
☎ 773/486-2700. Bowling

The Flat Iron, 52.
1565 N Milwaukee Ave
☎ 773/365-9000. Bar

The Globe Pub , 7.
1934 W Irving Park Rd
☎ 773/871-3757. British Pub

Gorilla Tango, 47.
1919 N Milwaukee Ave
☎ 773/598-4549. Comedy

Green Dolphin Street, 44.
2200 N Ashland Ave ☎ 773/395-0066.
Jazz/Latin

Green Mill, 3. 4802 N Broadway
☎ 773/878-5552. Jazz

Harry Caray's Tavern, 15.
3551 N Sheffield Ave
☎ 773/327-7800. Sports Bar

The Hideout, 55. 1354 W Wabansia
Ave ☎ 773/227-4433. Country

Holiday Club, 53. 4000 N Sheridan
Rd ☎ 773/348-9600. Lounge

Hopleaf, 4. 5148 N Clark St
☎ 773/334-9851. Bar

Hungry Brain, 31. 2319 W Belmont St
☎ 773/935-2118. Jazz

Hydrate, 21. 3458 N Halsted St
☎ 773/975-9244. Gay

I.O., 16. 3541 N Clark St
☎ 773/880-0199. Improv Comedy

Joe's, 56. 940 W Weed St
☎ 337-3486. Sports/Music

Katerina's, 8. 1920 W Irving Park Rd
☎ 773/348-7592. Coffeehouse/Jazz

Kingston Mines, 37.
2548 N Halsted St
☎ 773/477-4646. Blues

Kopi, a Traveler's Cafe, 1.
5317 N Clark St ☎ 989-5674. Cafe

MAP 57

Lakeshore Theater, 64.
3175 N Broadway
☎ 773/472-3492. Comedy

Liar's Club, 43. 1665 W Fullerton Ave
☎ 773/665-1110. DJ/Live Music

The Map Room, 46. 1649 N Hoyne Ave
☎ 773/252-7636. Bar

Martyr's, 9. 3855 N Lincoln Ave
☎ 773/404-9494. Eclectic Live Music

Metro, 11. 3730 N Clark St
☎ 773/549-0203. Rock

Neo, 39. 2350 N Clark St
☎ 773/528-2622. Dance Club

Ohm, 49. 1958 W North Ave
☎ 773/278-4646. Dance Club

Phyllis' Musical Inn, 65.
1800 W Division St ☎
773/486-9862. Rock

The Pony, 28.
1638 W Belmont Ave
☎ 773/828-5055. Bar

Prop House, 64. 1675 N Elston Ave
☎ 773/486-2086. Dance Club

Rosa's Lounge, 45. 3420 W Armitage
Ave ☎ 773/342-0452. Blues

Roscoe's, 22. 3356 N Halsted St
☎ 773/281-3355. Gay/DJ

**Sangria Restaurant and
Tapas Bar, 57.**
901 W Weed St ☎ 266-1200. DJ/Latin

Schubas Tavern, 27.
3159 N Southport Ave
☎ 773/525-2508. Rock/Folk

Second City, 61. 1616 N Wells St
☎ 337-3992. Comedy

Seven Ten Lounge, 35.
2747 N Lincoln Ave
☎ 773/549-2695. Bowling

Sidetrack, 20. 3349 N Halsted St
☎ 773/477-9189. Gay/Lesbian/Video

Sluggers, 18. 3540 N Clark St
☎ 773/248-0055. Sports Bar

Smart Bar, 11. 3730 N Clark St
☎ 773/549-4140. Dance Club

Subterranean, 48. 2011 W North Ave
☎ 773/278-6600. Eclectic

Uncle Fatty's Rum Resort, 32.
2833 N Sheffield Ave ☎ 773/477-3661.
Tiki/Tropical

Uncommon Ground, 12.
1214 W Grace St
☎ 773/929-3680. Eclectic

Victory Liquors, 36.
2610 N Halsted St
☎ 773/348-5600. Sports

Webster's Wine Bar, 41.
1480 W Webster Ave
☎ 773/868-0608.

Wild Hare, 19. 3530 N Clark St
☎ 773/327-4273. Reggae/World Beat

Wise Fool's Pub, 40. 2270 N Lincoln
Ave ☎ 773/929-1300. Live Music

Xippo, 10. 3759 N Damen Ave
☎ 773/529-9135. Lounge

Zanies, 61. 1548 N Wells St
☎ 337-4027. Comedy

Zentra, 58. 923 W Weed St
☎ 787-0400. Dance Club

Notes